Personality
Puzzle

Personality Puzzle

Understanding the People You Work With

Florence Littauer
and
Marita Littauer

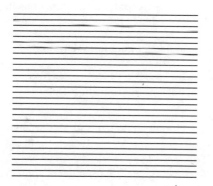

R Fleming H. Revell
A Division of Baker Book House
Grand Rapids, Michigan 49506

The personality summaries found on pages 201–204 are printed from *Personalities in Power,* by Florence Littauer, published by Huntington House, Inc., P. O. Box 53788, Lafayette, Louisiana 70505. The Personality Test Word Definitions found on pages 191–199 are adapted from *Personality Patterns* by Lana Bateman.

Library of Congress Cataloging-in-Publication Data

Littauer, Florence.
   Personality puzzle / Florence Littauer and Marita Littauer.
      p.   cm.
   ISBN 0-8007-1676-0
   1. Personality. 2. Temperament. 3. Characters and characteristics.
 I. Littauer, Marita. II. Title.
 BF698.3.L56 1992
 155.2′46—dc20
                                         92-5608
                                           CIP

Published by the Fleming H. Revell Company
Printed in the United States of America

Contents

Simple Tools
to Build a Better Life

In the twenty-five years that Fred and I have been speaking and writing on the four basic personalities, we have learned that if you can give people a tool so simple that they can quickly grasp it without sitting through special training and can put the information into use immediately, they will jump at an opportunity to use it. So many of us are walking through life with empty toolboxes hoping someone will give us some equipment that will work. Understanding the personalities works!

Initially, Fred and I started teaching couples in our home and used the personalities as a parlor game. We were astounded to see lives changed and marriages healed right before our eyes when people began to understand their inborn temperament traits and to realize that different isn't wrong. As they shared with friends the excitement of their new perceptions, we were asked to teach in churches and use the personalities as a tool to fulfill the scriptural admonition to examine ourselves. We taught many classes showing how to amplify our strengths and to work prayerfully and humanly to overcome our weaknesses but could not keep up with the demand. Ultimately Fred and I gave up other employment to work full time in helping people to understand themselves and others. We have always kept our teaching consistent with God's word and have seen the fruit of our labors as the Lord has blessed thousands with new insight on how to analyze themselves and get along with others.

When we don't have a way to understand people's personalities, we tend to judge others from our own perspective and to condemn them when they don't conform to our image. Oswald Chambers in his book *My Utmost for His Highest* writes,

> We are not true to one another as facts; we are true only to our ideas
> of one another. Everything is either delightful and fine, or mean and

dastardly according to our idea. We need to get to the point where we see men and women as they really are and yet there is no cynicism, we have no stinging, bitter things to say.

In order to see people as they really are and yet have no critical, stinging, bitter things to say, we need to understand the basic personality patterns and realize these other people are not "out to get us." They just see life from a different point of view.

I have written books applying the personality principles to marriage, difficult people, family relationships, politicians, depression, and childhood trauma. People have been asking for years, "When are you going to write a book about the use of personalities in business?" Here it is.

Personality Puzzle will help you to put the pieces together in your workplace or in any type of group activity where you have to relate to people who don't seem to see things your way.

Fred and I have been speaking to diverse groups—church conferences, medical and dental conventions, network marketing motivational meetings, and others—and we have learned that everyone is looking for simple tools to solve complex problems. Our daughter Marita grew up understanding the personalities from an early age, and she has been teaching them to office staffs, meeting planners, and church leaders, as well as coordinating the staff in our ministry office.

We have put our experiences and knowledge together in this book so that we can place simple tools into your toolbox that you may have the equipment to build an even better life for yourself, your family, and your coworkers.

Scripture tells us, "If possible, so far as it depends on you, be at peace with all men" (Romans 12:18 NAS).

When we understand the pieces of the puzzle we can be at peace with all people.

With Love, Joy, and Peace,

Florence Littauer
Lake San Marcos, CA
Summer 1992

Gentle Scrub Sponges.   X-39.10-A1   10/#4.99

Nature Shower Hand Soap (1)   5.00

Lipstick - Rose Silk.   10.00

                             ‾‾‾‾‾
                             29.99

Shampoo - dandruff
conditioner   "
2 Hand & Body Lotion

Night cream
Moisturizer
Foundation . Honey Cream
Hair spray

Seeing the Big Picture

Do you remember as a child how excited you got when you received a brand new puzzle? Perhaps it was a birthday or Christmas present or perhaps the gift was from a generous parent or friend. The box was sealed so you knew all the pieces were there. There would be no holes in your puzzle.

Some of you ripped open the box the quickest way possible, held it up high and giggled as the pieces fell in piles on the table. You loved doing the faces and the flowers, but you lost interest if there was too much sky or if no one wanted to do the puzzle with you.

Some of you got a sharp knife to cut the tape so you could open the box neatly. You tipped the box over gently and wouldn't think of starting the puzzle until you had analyzed the situation and divided the pieces into appropriate sections. You pulled out all the edge pieces and did those first so you would have a frame. You developed a system, placed pieces carefully, and would sulk for the rest of the day if little brother reached in and messed up your process.

Some of you grabbed the box away from your slower siblings, opened it quickly, and told the others what they were to do. "You find all the soldiers, you look for all the mountains. . . ." You got so enthused over the challenge of taking what appeared to be a hopeless mess and turning it into a beautiful picture that you scared off some of your more timid playmates and ended up doing the puzzle alone.

Some of you stared at the cover picture for a while, hoping the whole procedure would be simpler if you absorbed the expected result. You wanted to take your time and do the puzzle when you felt like it, but your older sister called you a slowpoke and took all the fun out of it. After a while you backed up, let the others take over, and decided, "This whole thing is too much like work."

Does one of these four sound something like you? Are you the Popular Sanguine who wants everything to be fun, but has a short attention span?

Or the Perfect Melancholy who believes that anything worth doing is worth doing right?

Or the Powerful Choleric who wants to be in charge and gets upset when people don't see it your way?

Or the Peaceful Phlegmatic who would rather not play if it's going to cause problems?

When we look back at the differences we had as children in approaching something as simple as putting together a puzzle, we can begin to understand the problems we face as we enter our workplace each day. Some people come in hoping to have fun; some play strictly by the rules and are inflexible; some tell everyone else what to do, even if they're not in charge; and some compromise consistently if it will avoid conflict.

How can we ever understand all of these various personalities?

Perhaps if we could remove the roof of our office, shop, school, church, hospital, or meeting place and really look inside, we would see something resembling a large box of scrambled puzzle pieces. Each one has its place, but it takes someone to put it all together and make sense of it. Each interlocking piece has strengths and weaknesses, parts that round out and parts that are indented. Some are right side up, others upside down, and a few pieces may even be stuck together, but when you look at the overall picture, you can see that just dumping them out of the box doesn't put the puzzle together. There's work to be done. Each piece is cut out to do a specific job; its colors and interlocking parts allow it to fit properly in only one location. A blue piece of sky may have what looks like the correct shape, but if we try to force it into the red flower area, the puzzle will never resemble the picture on the cover.

So it is in your workplace. The many people you work with day to day came into the box with certain strengths and weaknesses. There may be peaceful bits of azure sky, bright dots of flower faces, straight edges that form a side frame, and corner pieces that hold everything together. As we look at our workplace as a giant puzzle, we can see that all the different pieces are necessary to make the picture complete.

Some may be more appealing than others, but as we learn to identify and sort out the different personalities, we can appreciate their proper part in the picture. Our work environment and productivity can improve when we realize that rather than being a diverse collection of people tossed into a box, we can be pieced together like a perfect picture puzzle.

Whether you are the leader of the team or a part of the team, understanding how to put the Personality Puzzle together will make your time at work more enjoyable. You will soon look forward to going to work and will see each day as an adventure.

Some of us leave difficult workplaces or our homes only to attend frustrating volunteer meetings where the people are more challenging than those in our daily lives. We may all have one common goal or common interest, such as improving our children's schools or selecting the wallpaper for the ladies' room at our church, but we all arrive at the meeting with different ideas about how to achieve that goal or even about what the big picture should look like once we've put it together. This book will help us all to sort out and identify various personalities in any group situation so we can fit together the pieces in that great Personality Puzzle of life.

Who Is to Blame?

Bonnie came to our Personality Plus seminar and received a working knowledge of the four personalities. She knows that the Popular Sanguine is outgoing, optimistic, and fun loving. The Perfect Melancholy is detail conscious and a creative genius. The Powerful Choleric is a born leader who loves to be in charge. The Peaceful Phlegmatic is congenial and balanced, loves peace, and fears confrontation. Bonnie used the personalities with her friends and family, but she had not thought of applying the principles in her workplace. Bonnie owned a landscaping business that seemed to be doing well. The retail store was busy and there was a list of clients waiting for estimates for major landscaping jobs.

The Popular Sanguine salesman Jim was charming and well-liked, and the Perfect Melancholy designer Roger was meticulous and creative. The Peaceful Phlegmatic/Perfect Melancholy bookkeeper Harry paid the bills, wrote paychecks, caused her no problems, and hardly ever emerged from his tiny office. As a Powerful Choleric combined with Popular Sanguine herself, Bonnie liked to be in charge and also have fun. As is typical of this combination, Bonnie was overcommitted and preoccupied with family pressures and civic philanthropies. In the beginning Bonnie had run the whole business herself, but as things fell into place she spent less and less time at the office. She came in a few times a week to energize the staff and let them know she was still the boss and was the one who signed their paychecks.

Bonnie made a good living from the business and all seemed to be going well until the day came when the bookkeeper Harry called Bonnie to say there was not enough money in the bank to make the payroll.

"What do you mean we're out of money?" Bonnie yelled.

"We just don't have any money left," Harry said simply and calmly.

"When did this happen? Why didn't you tell me?"

"I didn't want to bother you."

"Bother me! Bother me! I can't believe you didn't warn me."

The typical Powerful Choleric response to problems is to find the culprit, place the blame, take the necessary action, and move on. In this case the bookkeeper seemed to be the culprit. Bonnie's first thought was to fire Harry. He was obviously irresponsible if he let things get this far out of hand. Let's get rid of him, bring in a new person, and tell him to straighten out the books.

The Popular Sanguine salesman Jim knew how to play to Bonnie's emotional needs. He commiserated with her, agreeing that the bookkeeper "holed away in that little corner" was out of touch with reality.

Roger, the Perfect Melancholy designer, was disheartened. He had been doing his work faithfully and thought everything was going well. He couldn't believe that the business had run out of money. His slightly suspicious side wondered if perhaps Harry had embezzled company funds. When he mentioned this to Bonnie, she grabbed onto the possibility. She was ready to accuse Harry and call the police. Luckily a Peaceful Phlegmatic friend had come to the business with Bonnie that day. She cautioned Bonnie not to jump to conclusions but to sit down with Harry and ask him what he perceived the cause of the problem to be. Who is to blame?

Poor Harry was close to tears by the time Bonnie turned up in his little office. He had heard the previous discussions and accusations through the walls. He knew he was about to be fired. And while he knew he wasn't guilty of embezzling, things had gotten so out of hand that he actually feared he might have to face a trial and jail.

To answer Bonnie's "Why didn't you warn me?" Harry explained that Bonnie never talked to him or even seemed interested in what he was doing. He said he felt alone and rejected because when Bonnie came into the office she spent her time with Jim who was fun and flattering and with Roger who always had creative landscaping designs to show her. Bonnie was stopped in her tracks when the reality of Harry's remarks hit her. She hated bookkeeping, found Harry to be dull and uninspiring, and avoided going into that tiny windowless office. She suddenly realized she hadn't given him or his work the time of day.

She was further stunned when Harry said, "Every time I tried to discuss the finances with you, you would ask 'Do we have enough money to make the payroll?' When I said we did, you'd say 'Then don't bother me with the details.' When the day came that we didn't have enough, I let you know."

Suddenly Harry wasn't such a bad guy. Bonnie finally understood that her flip comments about the payroll had been taken seriously by a serious man. She didn't realize how her dislike of details and "dreary people" had caused her to avoid learning the truth. As long as she got her paycheck each week, she had no desire to look for trouble. And she had, without realizing it, taught her staff that she only wanted to hear good news. Cage up those bad news bears!

She sank down into the chair, relaxed her tense body, and forced herself to ask calmly, "How did we get into this situation?" Bonnie dreaded a lengthy, complicated fiscal explanation that she might not understand. As the boss she didn't want to look stupid. If she were totally honest with herself, that was why she had not asked questions before.

Harry said, "It's really very simple. Jim is a great salesman who charms everyone into redoing their entire yard. Roger designs the plan, and it looks wonderful. Jim underestimates the cost; Roger overdoes the plan. When customers see how expensive the job is becoming they either call a halt to it and refuse to pay or they complain to Jim. Jim can't stand people being mad at him so he agrees to do the job at the estimated price, which means we lose money. So what you have here is a creative and charming staff that is very busy losing your money."

Now Bonnie was ready to fire Jim and Roger, but instead she gave us a call. When she told us her plight, she explained that suddenly her knowledge of the Personality Puzzle hit her. She had never thought of using this information in her business. Her own Powerful Choleric personality wanted to be in charge and see the big picture, but she avoided what to her seemed petty and dull. The Popular Sanguine part of her was more interested in her social activities than the discipline of daily routine. She had let everyone know that she didn't want to hear the negatives, so her staff fed her only what would keep her happy.

Bonnie realized she had been out having fun and hadn't been in charge at all. She had let the whole business drift on its own while thinking her periodic visits to cheer everybody on exhibited control. Her staff knew how to handle her. They complimented her appearance and showed her how much work they were doing. Only Harry had not played the game, and because of his financial focus, she had avoided him.

Once Bonnie saw the error of her ways and was willing to work on herself instead of asking whom she should blame, the solutions came quickly. We helped her to see how to correct her situation. She had to make sure each person was functioning in his strengths and not his weaknesses, and she had to hold each one to honest accountability. In the new plan, Jim used his outgoing personality to make initial contact with the potential customers and to excite them over the horticultural horizons for their home. When it was time for the estimate, Roger went with Jim. Together they offered realistic options with the dollar signs attached to each possibility. In this way the customer had choices without negative surprises. When confronted, Jim admitted he had guessed at estimates without any practical basis. Roger agreed that he had overdesigned without regard to Jim's estimates.

There was no one person to blame for the financial problems of what appeared to be a thriving business. It was a compilation of circumstances where the pieces of the puzzle did not make a pretty picture. To fit everything together and put the pieces in place, Bonnie had to get to work and become the leader she fancied herself to be. She had to come in each morning on schedule, be a disciplined example to the others, and not let her social life and philanthropies stand in the way of fiscal responsibility. Harry had to give Bonnie simple and clear weekly financial statements. And she had to force herself to read them. Before giving away trees and plants to customers who complained, Jim had to check with Bonnie who forced herself to call and hear the complaint firsthand. Almost all the problems were solved instantly when people realized they were talking to the boss. Bonnie learned it was better to face issues quickly herself than to let them multiply through neglect.

Business is improving; Bonnie is disciplined and really in charge. Harry is getting credit for his quiet behind the scenes work and has been given a bigger office with a window. Jim is having fun charming the clients. And Roger is being artistic, creative, and more realistic about his decisions while holding Jim to accountability.

By using her knowledge of the Personality Puzzle, Bonnie was able to keep all her staff and to appreciate their differences. Each one of them began to function in his strengths and not his weaknesses. They all, including Bonnie, acted rationally rather than overreacting and ruining a potentially prosperous business.

We hope that, like Bonnie, as you read this book and learn to put the pieces together in your workplace, you will be working in your areas of strength to create a prosperous and peaceful business. In this book we will look at the different personalities and see how to piece them together for a harmonious and productive workplace. First we will look at the *visible* pieces of each person's personality. Each personality type has certain behavior patterns, ways of dressing, and even posture that make it easy to identify which piece they are without analyzing them or submitting them to psychological testing. You can identify the people you work with, and they don't even need to know you have figured them out!

Once you have identified each piece as Bonnie did, you need to understand the *various* characteristics that make up each personality. You will learn about their strengths and weaknesses and how they relate to the workplace. Through the stories and examples of others you will begin to see each person you work with for who *they* are rather than who *you* are.

Remember the Golden Rule, "Do unto others as you would have them do unto you"? Most of us were brought up on its logic, and it makes good sense when we are talking about morals and ethics. But when it comes to getting along with others, the Golden Rule is tarnished. For those purposes, it should read, "Do unto others as *they* would have you do unto *them*." This is the secret of relationship success. With all the various personalities we encounter every day, we need skills and help to give them what they want. Because all people have different needs and desires according to their own personalities, we have to learn how to meet these needs.

Once we've figured out that we can see people's personality types and that they are various, it's a logical step for us to learn the basic desires and emotional needs of the people in our workplaces. These *valuable* pieces of information enable us to not only understand the people we work with, but also to get along with them and make all of our lives easier.

Putting together the *visible, various,* and *valuable* pieces will solve the Personality Puzzle of each workplace, and going to work will become more and more fun!

Personality Puzzle

PART ONE

The Visible Pieces of the Puzzle

How to Recognize the Personalities in Your Workplace

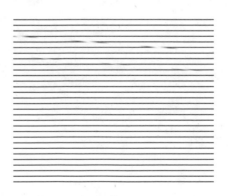

CHAPTER 1

The Whole Picture Is Made Up of Many Pieces

Business shelves are bursting with books offering tips on managing, marketing, and presentation skills. Among them seems to be an abundance of new ways to test people's personalities. Some are complex and require trained professionals with complete computer analysis systems to administer them. Others are simple question and answer quizzes.

When Chuck, Marita's husband, was in graduate school getting his master's degree in marriage and family counseling, he took a class called "Assessment." The purpose of this class was to educate the future therapists on the various testing tools available to them. Chuck constantly brought home new tests for Marita to take. For some, she had to use a number two pencil and fill in the little bubble completely. Others required choosing a response: "Very much like me," "Not at all like me," or "I'm not sure." When the endless stream of testing was finished and the computerized reports came back, they all said the same thing: Marita is what the early Greek thinkers would have called a Sanguine/Choleric. The tests labeled her with an alphabet soup jumble of letters, none of which made much sense to her or was easy to remember. But they all boiled down to the fact that Marita likes to have fun more than anything else, and she likes to be in control. While the various tests may use different labels, your results on any of them should pinpoint the same basic characteristics, because those traits are who you are. In the chart on the next page we have listed just a few of the most popular systems in comparison with the original terms which we use in all of our personality books.

Getting Along with Others

With so much already available it might seem foolish to write yet another book to help analyze a person's personality. Yet, *Personality Puzzle* gives you a simple tool that will allow you to quickly and easily identify the basic personality traits of those with whom you work in your career or volunteer activities. Once you understand how they function, you will have more realistic expectations of their work styles and emotional needs.

Getting along with coworkers is an increasingly important skill. A survey of the top three traits employers preferred in employees revealed a surprising top pick. Eighty-four percent of the respondents included good interpersonal skills. Only 40 percent included education and experience among their top three (*Executive Female Magazine,* May/June 1991, page 12). Getting along with others in the workplace is an important necessity for all of us!

Personality Puzzle Comparison Chart

Personality Puzzle	Popular Sanguine	Powerful Choleric	Perfect Melancholy	Peaceful Phlegmatic
Larry Crabb	Emotional	Volitional	Rational	Personal
Gary Smalley & John Trent	Otter	Lion	Beaver	Golden Retriever
Personal Profile System	Influencing	Dominance	Cautious	Steadiness
Alessandra & Cathcart	Socializer	Director	Thinker	Relater
Merrill-Reid Social Styles	Expressive	Driving	Analytical	Amiable

SOURCES:
The Training Manual by Lawrence J. Crabb, Jr. Ph.D. (Institute of Biblical Counseling, 1978).
Gary Smalley and John Trent, *The Two Sides of Love* (Focus on the Family Publishers, 1990), pp. 34–36.
Carlson Learning Company
Anthony Alessandra and Jim Cathcart, *Relationship Strategies* (Nightingale-Conant, 1990).
Merrill-Reid, Social Styles, "How Do They Manage" by Susan Fletcher (*American Way Magazine,* October 1982), pp. 192–194.

Finding a Simple System

Back in the times of the ancient Greek philosophers, Hippocrates, the father of modern medicine, started observing his patients. He found that while no two people were exactly alike, many had similar characteristics. One group often shared certain consistent behavior patterns. On the other hand, other groups exhibited extremely different sets of behavior, although they acted consistently within their group. Once Hippocrates and his coworkers observed which group a person fit into, they could accurately predict other aspects of the person's responses to life. They called those whose obvious traits were being loud and late, were optimistic, and loved to have fun Sanguines. They called those who loved to be the leaders of the pack and tended toward bossiness Cholerics. The ones who needed to have all of life in order and were moodier than the others were named Melancholies. And finally they designated the people who preferred to watch and who could easily go in any direction as long as someone else made the choice Phlegmatics.

Hippocrates originally felt that each group behaved as it did because of certain bodily fluids. The word *Sanguine* means blood and is related to high energy and optimism. *Choleric* is yellow bile, which is connected to control and anger. *Melancholy* represented black bile and was chosen because of the person's depth of intelligence and tendency toward depression. *Phlegmatic* comes from bodily phlegm, which keeps the person peaceful, passive, and stolid. Long ago medical science dropped that aspect of Hippocrates' analysis. But the behavioral observations have remained so valid over the years that the majority of personality studies have their roots in Hippocrates' theory of the four temperament patterns even though they may have changed the labels to Socializer or Otter.

In keeping with the original ideas we will use the same terms, *Sanguine, Choleric, Melancholy,* and *Phlegmatic.* To make these terms easier for you to remember, we have added a descriptive word to each. We will refer to Popular Sanguines, Powerful Cholerics, Perfect Melancholies, and Peaceful Phlegmatics. Together they make up the complete picture of the Personality Puzzle. The bright flowers are Popular Sanguines; Powerful Cholerics are the corners that hold everything together; Perfect Melancholies form the frame of straight edge pieces; Peaceful Phlegmatics fill the blue sky.

The early observers didn't have computers to analyze results for them. They didn't have the high-tech testing we have today. And yet, by simply watching people's behavior, they developed concepts that are woven throughout all of our complicated quizzes. Some of the newer systems in the study of personality may be more complete or give a more complex rundown of every characteristic. Some of them require a willing participant and a costly consultation. But we wish to present a simple tool. We have learned that when you can give people a tool so simple that they can use its benefits immediately, their lives will change for the better.

Before you proceed with reading this book, turn to Appendix A: Your Personality Profile, page 186. Take a few minutes to complete the profile and read the directions for interpreting it. Doing this will give you a tool for fitting yourself into the *visible, various,* and *valuable* pieces of the Puzzle.

Being Alert to Life

In leadership seminars, called CLASS, we teach people the value of the Personality Puzzle and how they can open their eyes to the people around them. So many of us never look to see what's happening on either side of us, yet all successful people have a pulse beat on the people surrounding them. We call this being "alert to life." We encourage everyone to make a habit of observing people and tuning in to what's going on in their personal arena. We receive many letters back from CLASS attendees telling us they didn't know how much they were missing until they became alert to life. After attending CLASS, Shirley wrote,

> The most penetrating lesson that continues to accompany me daily is the "alert to life" lesson. What exciting things have opened up for me, and with the additional lesson on the Personality Puzzle, I am not only aware of life around me but I am no longer confined by my Popular Sanguine weaknesses. Instead I am discovering exciting new opportunities to turn weaknesses into strengths. My world has really expanded intellectually, which seemed unattainable for me . . . without a degree!
>
> Florence taught me lessons too numerous to relate without writing a book (I haven't accomplished that goal yet, but I will!!). However, I believe the key teaching for me was an "alertness to life." The knowledge God has given Florence and her willingness to pass it on to me has been an inspiration. This thought is stated best in Proverbs 27:17, "Iron sharpens iron, and one person sharpens the wits of another." She has accomplished this through her own speaking and sharing and through the talents of her staff.

Marita was my small group leader, and she was exactly what I needed. I have the same personality that she has, both a combination of Popular Sanguine and Powerful Choleric, and I saw how she functioned within that temperament by using her creativity and leadership skills. She was also very helpful in answering my questions and encouraging me concerning my goals and dreams.

No matter what your goals and dreams maybe, being alert to life and understanding the Personality Puzzle will move you more quickly up the ladder of success and show you how, as you are alert to those around you, to understand those who are nothing like you.

What do you do when you've got a boss who assigns you a project and then forgets to ever ask for it? Or, a colleague whose obsessive attention to detail is holding a whole project back? Or, an employee whose continued procrastination is damaging client relations?

You might be able to send them off for testing or bring in a consultant to clear up the confusion. That would all take time, training, and money. Or like the originators of this entire concept, you could observe those around you. Based on watching their behavior patterns, you can get a better understanding of where they fit into the whole picture. You can learn what to expect from them, what they'll need in order to function their best, and, most important, how to get along with them.

These people you are observing don't need to take a long test and you don't need to have it computer analyzed. In fact, they don't even need to know you are learning to understand them. Just watch and you will see.

CHAPTER 2

Popular Sanguines:
The Bright Flowers in Your Puzzle

We like to start with Popular Sanguines because as the bright flowers in the Personality Puzzle they are the easiest to spot. They are the ones who stand out in almost any crowd.

Bright Clothing

The most obvious way to spot Popular Sanguines is by their brightly colored or dramatic clothing. There are exceptions to every rule, but, given a choice, a Popular Sanguine woman will often wear fashionable and even trendy clothing. Or maybe she'll choose large earrings that wiggle when she walks if her workplace allows such creative touches. A Popular Sanguine man may wear a bright, almost flamboyant tie, a boldly striped shirt, or perhaps a colored sport coat in a mostly gray-suit environment.

If you haven't seen the movie *The Accidental Tourist,* or if it's been a while, rent it and watch for the various personality styles. William Hurt plays a Peaceful Phlegmatic, Macon Leary, who writes travel books for businessmen who hate to travel, as he does. He and his Powerful Choleric wife separate through the grief surrounding the death of their son. He is left with the dog and now has to find someone to take care of the dog while he continues his travels. The person he finds is an obvious Popular Sanguine personality named Muriel, played by Geena Davis. Muriel boards dogs and teaches obedience classes, so her job allows for flexible dressing. She wears flowing, brightly colored, gauzy dresses with jingling belts and dangling earrings. Her lipstick is red and matches her long polished fingernails. Watching this movie is a study in personalities and how they interact.

Popular Sanguines are naturally attracted to reds, bright pinks, turquoise, and royal blue, and they love large prints and showy flowers. The look that combines several compatible but dissimilar prints into one outfit, such as a plaid, a floral, and a stripe of coordinating colors, appeals to Popular Sanguine's taste for a unique style. They never want to enter a room unnoticed.

While this extreme fashion sense is more true of women than men, a Popular Sanguine man will usually try for some creativity and color in his clothing.

Intriguing Personality

We think Kathie Lee Gifford of "LIVE—with Regis and Kathie Lee" is an obvious Popular Sanguine. Each morning she amuses all her viewers as she gestures wildly and winks into the camera as if she were looking straight at you and you alone. Her hair is stylishly wild, her eyes are wide and innocent, and her outfits defy description. Her mouth is always open, and what comes out is beyond predictability. Regis Philbin, her partner, seems to be the Perfect Melancholy opposite, looking as if he's constantly appalled at her lack of discretion and bodily contortions. He seems embarrassed to be on the set with her.

On the morning *People* magazine unveiled its "Twenty-Five Most Intriguing People of 1991," Regis held the magazine in its plain brown wrapper and wondered aloud if he had made the list. "I'm deep and mysterious," he said. "That's what makes me intriguing."

Kathie, perched precariously on a high stool, leaned dangerously forward and asked the camera, "Do you think I'm on the list?"

Regis immediately countered, "You? Intriguing? You who have laid your entire life out before the world over and over again? There's nothing left we don't know about you. There's no mystery in you."

Kathie rose to the bait and gave the dramatic Popular Sanguine hurt look—hand to her head, her eyes blinking back little tears, and mouth hanging open in shock at what she'd heard.

She quickly recovered, and with a defiant toss of her head she shot back, "Well at least I can take it if I don't make the list. I'm ready to accept it, but you won't be able to handle it. You'll be depressed for weeks." Regis dropped his head into his hands and gave us a "woe is me" look.

Sadly enough, neither one made the list.

Loud Voices

Another way to know there are Popular Sanguines in the room is by the noise level. They have naturally loud voices. In a setting where they are comfortable, they may enter the room with a loud cheerful greeting that bears their hallmark style such as "What a great day it is today!" Marita greets her staff with, "Hello! Hello! Hello!" Popular Sanguines like to be noticed and don't mind being known for their unique greeting style.

In addition to volume, most Popular Sanguines also have a great deal of vocal variety and modulation. If a group of them go somewhere together, everyone will know they are there. Our CLASS seminar staff encompasses a variety of personality types, but many of us are Popular Sanguines. When we go out to eat together, we try to request a private room or an out of the way section so we don't disturb the other diners. If we are put into the main area, we often notice that we have become the central focus of the restaurant because of our loud and constant conversation. Sometimes we are scowled at; other times fellow Populars who have been envying our fun will stop by and join in with the chatter.

Popular Sanguines often say whatever comes to their minds without first thinking. If you understand they are innocent and don't mean anything harmful, you can take it when they say, as one woman said to Florence, "Your hair looks so much better than it did the last time—it was kind of floozy like." Florence could either have done research on how she had her hair the last time or laugh it off—which is what she chose to do.

Popular Sanguines tend to dominate conversations. They answer questions asked of others, without even realizing what they have done. One day Marita noticed she was guilty of this. She was sitting alone in her office working on a project when she heard one staff member ask another a question. It had no relationship to what she was working on, but before anyone else could offer an answer to the question, Marita hollered the answer through her open door into the larger office area. When she heard herself interjecting her thoughts into someone else's conversation, she laughed, thinking the behavior was cute. Popular Sanguines think even their weaknesses are adorable.

Another obvious conversational habit of Popular Sanguines is their quick pace. Their rapid-fire style of speaking usually comes from their natural enthusiasm for their topic. Or they may fear that if they pause for a moment someone else might jump in, that they will lose their conversational lead, or that the listener will have to leave before they finish their lengthy and hilarious story. Through the fear of losing their audience, they will often physically hold on to the listener and maintain close eye contact.

Grand Gestures

From a distance you may not be able to hear their conversation, but you can still observe Popular Sanguines' style by their expansive gestures. Even if they are on the telephone or talking to themselves, Popular Sanguines will freely flail their hands for emphasis. Recently Marita observed a Popular Sanguine man using his cellular phone in an airport waiting area. She was just passing by, but her attention was drawn to the crowded waiting area by the loud voice that she heard above the airport noise. She saw a man, sport coat off, leaning back in his seat with his legs crossed in such a way that they occupied both his seat and the one next to him. His cellular phone was held to his ear by his shoulder and his arms were moving with his conversation. Of course, the person on the other end of the phone didn't need the gestures, and it's doubtful the caller was even aware of what he was doing.

It is not uncommon for Popular Sanguines to get so engrossed in a conversation that they forget there are others around them. They will be gesturing wildly as someone walks by, and the innocent passerby is apt to get belted across the chest. If you see someone conversing with expansive gestures and you are holding something you wouldn't want spilled on you, be sure to stay out of the way.

Casual Order at Work

Popular Sanguines' workspace reflects their casual style. Their desks are typically cluttered with papers and piles. Other personalities look at the disaster on Popular Sanguines' desks and wonder how they can function with so many different projects piling up on one another. Yet Popular Sanguines can usually put their hands on a particular paper at a moment's notice.

Among the papers and projects there is apt to be an interesting collection of personal paraphernalia. It may include birthday cards from months earlier, a little teddy bear or other cute toy that someone gave them, several pictures of their family (including the dog), and flowers or a wilted plant. There may be crumbs or other food remnants. And occasionally papers will have splash marks from spilled coffee. Hanging from the corner of a picture frame there may be name tags as a reminder of last year's conventions.

Popular Sanguines' drawers may be fairly nonfunctional. They put everything they need out on the desk or they forget about it. Drawers are used to catch clutter, and, therefore, they have very little organization. Files may be alphabetized, but casually. The A's are usually together but the second letter of the word is likely to be out-of-order. They work better with colored file folders and will more quickly remember that a needed paper is in a green file than what title it was filed under. The files themselves may be thick with papers including duplicate copies and outdated notes. Papers may be facing in different directions, and some are probably sticking out.

Since Popular Sanguines are visually stimulated, they don't do well with typical "in" boxes or schedule books. Things have a tendency to get buried in an "in" box and never get dealt with.

One of Marita's clients is the founder and director of a successful Christian counseling center. She FAXed him some important papers that needed quick response. When she hadn't heard from him in several days she phoned him. He said he hadn't seen the FAXes but thought maybe they got put in his "in" drawer. While she was on the phone he looked. Yes, there they were along with mail and other new items that had come in for him. He laughed and explained that his "in" box was overflowing so badly that he decided to put it all into one of his unused drawers. The problem was, now it was truly out of sight and out of mind. Now if Marita sends him a FAX, she writes across the cover page with a bold marker, "Do not put this in Gaylen's 'in' drawer. Hand it to him when he comes in!" So far this approach has worked.

Place a note in the center of the desk on top of the piles or hand deliver it directly to Popular Sanguine and it has a higher chance of being noticed. To remind themselves of important appointments, Popular Sanguines do better to leave themselves large notes where they will see them every day rather than listing appointments in a schedule book. Post-it Notes are a boon to Popular Sanguines as they can stick them everywhere as reminders. Placing papers that need to be taken home on the floor in the doorway is safer than putting them in an easily ignored "out" box.

While this casual style of work environment may seem distracting to other personalities, it enhances Popular Sanguines' creative ability and truly makes them more productive.

Spotting Ads Aimed at Popular Sanguines

Besides observing people in real life, movies, or books, you can practice the Personality Puzzle by watching commercials and reading ads. From now on when you look at advertising, ask yourself what personality would be attracted to this particular pitch. In the chapters in Part One that describe the personality types, we'll offer some different kinds of ad appeal. When you peruse ads, be sure to pay attention to the kinds of words used and to the advertised benefit to the consumer. We think you'll enjoy the challenge of spotting the different personalities in ads you see every day.

Popular Sanguines love ads that promise fun, escape, and excitement. Wanderlusting Popular Sanguines are, for instance, the ones who most often make vacation travel arrangements. Powerful Cholerics consider vacations a waste of productive time, Perfect Melancholies have to weigh the price against the pleasure, and Peaceful Phlegmatics can't decide where to go.

Ads for cruises that offer indulgence and use words like *fabulous, fantastic, endless opportunities,* and *enthralling* entice Popular Sanguines. Other vacations that promise endless activities, friendly locals, and a thrill a minute appeal to Popular Sanguines while they may seem trivial to Powerful Cholerics and worldly to Perfect Melancholies. Peaceful Phlegmatics get tired just thinking about them.

Popular Sanguines like to buy gifts for others. They want everybody to share the fun. They'll often be attracted to gimmicks and toys that whir, move, sing, or dance—gifts that may or may not appeal to their recipients. Since Popular Sanguines like to receive gifts even more than they like to give them, they'll be most tempted to respond to ads that offer them a present as well. Direct mail advertising often uses this technique. Any "free gift for ordering now" offer will appeal to a Popular Sanguine, especially if the free gift is a frivolous item. (Free gift incentives might also appeal to practical Perfect Melancholies, but they'd be suspicious of getting something for nothing.)

Look at Me

Begin to pay attention to yourself and the people in your work life. Some of you will see yourself in this description of the Popular Sanguine. Now you know why your office is a mess. You may want to throw away your schedule book and get yourself some large multicolored Post-it Notes.

Some of you probably felt peeved when you read the description of Popular Sanguines' loud clothing and louder voices. You may well have wondered why certain people in your office *always* need to have people notice them. Now you know. You can begin to use this information tomorrow. Those people aren't attracting attention to themselves to annoy you. They aren't trying to hog all the credit. They're simply being their Popular Sanguine selves. Simply knowing that can make them easier to deal with.

Read on, and you'll know more about each of the personalities, including which one you are.

CHAPTER 3

Perfect Melancholies:
The Straight Edges in Your Puzzle

Next to Popular Sanguines' loud demeanor and dress, Perfect Melancholies are the easiest to spot in a crowd. They are the straight-edge pieces in the Personality Puzzle.

Conservative Clothing

The key to observing the Perfect Melancholy is the word *perfect*. Everything about them will be perfect and tidy, with the minor exception of the "absent-minded professor" type of Melancholy, who is so intellectual that he or she can't be bothered by appearances. You can quickly identify most Perfect Melancholies by their clothing, posture, and hair style, which will generally be neat and close to the head. A Perfect Melancholy woman tends to wear her hair in a straighter style, either neatly pulled back or in a blunt cut. If she has permed or curly hair, it will be in a conservative style. A Perfect Melancholy man has every hair in place and will look as if he's overdosed on hair spray.

At our local grocery store there are several managers but two of them stand out through their extreme personalities, and their fashion sense follows accurately.

Tom is a Perfect Melancholy and Jack a Popular Sanguine. Tom is a small-framed man with proper little wire-rimmed glasses and has every hair in place. His required blue shirt is set off with a repeated pattern red tie and is always perfectly pressed and tightly tucked in as if he were in the military. His pants have a neat crease, and his shoes have a polished shine. He walks with perfect posture and makes small, precise gestures as he talks.

Then there is Jack, immediately noticeable by the large and colorful flowers on his tie, which provide his Popular Sanguine touch of rebellion to the traditional uniform. Jack chats happily with the customers and will often holler across four check stands to say hello to a frequent shopper. His shirt, while not a disaster, doesn't have the crispness of Tom's, and it is only loosely tucked in. Jack's hair is neat but has a more natural and casual feeling. You don't need to talk to these two managers to determine which personality they are. Just observing their dress and interacting styles will reveal two very different personalities.

Even Perfect Melancholies' casual clothes have that perfect look. One day Marita was visiting a Perfect Melancholy friend. Amy was ironing—a favorite Melancholy pastime. Marita was shocked as she watched! Amy turned the pair of casual slacks she was ironing inside out and carefully pressed the lining of the back pocket. When Marita commented on what she perceived to be excessive work, Amy said, "It lies smoothly this way." So logical to the Perfect Melancholy, yet ironing what doesn't show would never occur to Popular Sanguines unless they had a Perfect Melancholy parent who taught them perfect ironing techniques.

Most Perfect Melancholies are attracted to the more conservative colors, which will give you another clue to identifying a Perfect Melancholy by sight. Marita's perfect husband, Chuck, prefers gray and khaki. Although he may already have five pairs of khaki slacks, he still feels he has a need for another pair since some of those others are no longer "perfect." One year Marita, a Popular Sanguine, gave Chuck a pair of teal green slacks. Chuck says they are "bright" green and refuses to wear them. Once a year at Christmastime, Marita can convince Chuck to wear the "bright" green pants as a personal favor to her.

One slight exception to the color rule is when the Perfect Melancholy has an artistic bent and brightly colored clothing is highly fashionable. This will, of course, be more true of women than men, and their other perfect features will still reveal their true Perfect Melancholy personalities.

Another exception is the Perfect Melancholy man whose Popular Sanguine wife buys his clothes. One man we saw was wearing purple slacks and a purple paisley shirt. We assumed because of the loud colors that he was a Popular Sanguine. When we asked about his personality he replied, "My wife bought these and insisted I wear them. I'm actually a Perfect Melancholy. I'm humiliated to go out of the house like this so I pretend I'm in navy blue and don't look down."

Perfect Posture

Posture is another giveaway in identifying a Perfect Melancholy. While the Popular Sanguine's whole presence is rather loose and open, the Perfect Melancholy is more confined. The Perfect Melancholy person stands erectly and sits properly.

While eating lunch in a restaurant in South Carolina, Marita observed a man at the next table. He was obviously a Perfect Melancholy. He wore a crisp white long-sleeved shirt and a red tie. His perfect navy suit had proper pleats and neat cuffs. His flawlessly polished black loafers had both the tassel and kiltie giving them the perfect power look. He sat straight in his chair and occasionally rested his wrist on the edge of the table. Each hair was in place, and his mustache was perfectly trimmed.

You can expect Perfect Melancholies to stand up straight and make discreet gestures. While Popular Sanguines are apt to wave one arm as they hug someone with the other, Perfect Melancholies keep their hands close to their body and won't touch you unless you have a very close relationship with them. If you hug a Perfect Melancholy person you don't know very well, you may feel as though you have just hugged a board. Perfect Melancholies like their space and, in turn, won't invade yours.

Organized Workspace

The workspace of the Perfect Melancholy will, of course, look perfect and professional. In the Perfect Melancholy office, everything has its place. Files will hang neatly in Pendaflex folders. Papers will all face the same way and the folders will have neatly typed labels.

Chuck has matching file folders. When he no longer has a need for a particular folder, because it has a mark on it or the label is incorrect, he used to throw it away. When Marita saw these fresh-looking file folders in the trash, she retrieved them and took them to her office. Her attitude was that it saved money, and it's fun to find free folders in the trash. Now Chuck just gives them to her when he's done with them. He can't stand to reuse a folder by relabeling it and messing it up. She can't bear to throw good folders away.

One day Marita saw a little list on a Post-it Note on Chuck's desk. The list contained several unrelated items. When Marita questioned him, Chuck stated that it was his list of "things waiting to get on the list." He explained further by reaching into his file drawer and pulling out a perfect-looking file with one piece of paper in it. "This," he said, "is my inventory. There are sections for tools, audio equipment, sporting goods, photography gear, and computer supplies. When I buy something new I put it on this Post-it list until I have time to redo the inventory and include the new items. If I sell something, I also list it on the waiting list to be removed later." It all seemed "perfectly" logical to Chuck. A place for everything and everything in its place.

Perfect Melancholies' desks have only their current project on the top. When the day is over, Perfect Melancholies clear off their desks and put all their work away, leaving their desks neat and clean. Our Perfect Melancholy business manager, Karen, removes everything from her desktop every Monday, coats the desk with a fresh layer of furniture polish, makes the surface shine, and puts everything back where it belongs.

Perfect Melancholies do well with schedule books, "in" baskets, and other basic organizational tools. In fact, they often have highly categorized schedule books, with sections for meetings, appointments, reminders to run errands, work tasks they need to accomplish, leisure activities, and so on, and with each half hour accounted for.

Given a choice, Perfect Melancholies keep their drawers locked since they like privacy. But if you had an opportunity to look inside the desk drawers of the Perfect Melancholy you would find the pattern repeated. There's a place for everything. There may be a little paper clip holder, a pen and pencil holder, a special place for a ruler and scissors, extra lead and erasers for mechanical pencils, a pen refill, spare batteries. In addition to having a well-stocked desk, they know exactly what is there and where it is. If someone borrows something and forgets to put it back, Perfect Melancholies know the second they open their drawer exactly what is missing. They ask in a discouraged tone, "Who took my red pen this time?" Since Popular Sanguines often can't find their own supplies and need to borrow from others, they should be the first ones questioned when an item is discovered missing.

Personal touches in the Perfect Melancholies' workspaces are typically small and unobtrusive, perhaps a picture of the family and a trophy or two that connect to their profession. Florence's assistant, Irene, is a Perfect Melancholy. Her office contains all the things Florence doesn't know what to do with, neatly arranged in piles. Next to her phone is a tiny one by one-and-a-half inch photo of herself and her husband, Ralph.

Look around at the people in your life and your work. Those with proper posture and behavior, conservative clothing, and an overall neat and tidy appearance are most likely the Perfect Melancholies.

The words *impeccable, elegant, meticulous,* and *perfect* are often used to describe Giorgio Armani, the celebrated fashion designer. From a buyer in a Milan department store, he has risen to become one of the world's top designers with his own prestigious label. He heads an international fashion empire with estimated volume of sales of more than $600 million a year. It has been said that his sewing machines turned to gold.

Every step in his perfect life represents to us the Perfect Melancholy personality. He looks perfect, he moves gracefully, and he notices every detail. Approaching age sixty, Armani is movie-star handsome, svelte of form, and serious of purpose. He trains all of his staff to be his perfect clones, and he accepts nothing short of 100 percent effort and success. He is an avowed perfectionist in looks and actions. An article in *Forbes* magazine (28 Oct. 1991) says of Armani, "He is really a tightly wound man, a demanding micro manager who can explode if he finds a single thread out of place."

"My faults and my virtues are the same, whether as a designer or a businessman," says Armani in the same article. "Nothing is ever enough. I must check everything. It causes me problems—people think I don't trust anyone. But I must know what's going on."

Armani is the consummate Perfect Melancholy, a modern day Renaissance man.

Ads Aimed at Perfect Melancholies

Perfect Melancholies are not looking for fluffy fun or impulsive action but for depth, sensitivity, and perfection. They are the artistic geniuses, the computer whiz kids, the detail-conscious watchdogs. Their brand of fun is quiet and thoughtful analysis. They act only after careful consideration. An ad combining scenic beauty, proper perspective, and rewarding mastery can't fail to touch the deep emotions of the Perfect Melancholy.

The travel ads that most appeal to Perfect Melancholies are those that promise time to be introspective, to consider one's life and one's options. Perfect Melancholies like vacation opportunities that appeal to their intellect and promise to teach them something—study tours in Europe, for example. They also like ads that promise them that a trip can be exactly tailored to fit their needs. And, of course, they respond to price-saving features in travel ads.

Popular Sanguines respond to car ads that show red vehicles with lots of chrome and attractive people having fun with their new cars. Perfect Melancholies, on the other hand, like to know lots of details about the vehicle's brakes, torque systems, engine capability, and safety standards.

An ad for anything featuring lots of specific statistical information is likely to appeal to a Perfect Melancholy. This is stuff most Popular Sanguines couldn't be bothered to read—whether it's about phone systems, financial services, or clothing. Perfect Melancholies aren't likely to respond well to an investment house ad that says an agency will worry about details for them. Perfect Melancholies like to worry about their own details, thank you very much.

Perfect Melancholies are fascinated with electronic gadgets that most other types would never learn to operate—electronic notebooks or address books, watches that tell the time around the globe at the push of a button, pens with tape recorders in them.

The ads that are designed to be attractive to the Perfect Melancholy use precise wording such as "proper perspective," "rewarded with an understanding," "well-tailored suit," and "touch your very soul." You can touch the soul of Perfect Melancholies by speaking to them in their language and not wasting their time with trivia and baubles.

As you read or view promotional pieces in the future, pay special attention to the style of words that are used. They will give you a format to follow when you communicate with the various pieces of the Personality Puzzle.

CHAPTER 4

Powerful Cholerics: The Corners That Hold Your Puzzle Together

As the corner pieces of the Personality Puzzle, the ones who hold everything together in their tight grip, Powerful Choleric people are more concerned with function than fluff. While Popular Sanguines can be quickly spotted by their loud voices and flashy dress, and Perfect Melancholies are easily identified by their flawless appearance and proper demeanor, Powerful Cholerics can be spotted more through their pace than by their packaging.

Pace Not Packaging

Powerful Cholerics are strong, as is noted by their powerful description. If you were to stand on a busy street corner and just watch the people going by, you would spot the Popular Sanguines either happily chatting with friends or, if they are alone, scanning the crowd in hopes of finding someone to talk to or something exciting to do. Perfect Melancholies are the ones with straight posture and even paces. Then, walking faster than the rest and with a heavy foot, will be Powerful Cholerics. As they stride along you may feel the ground shake beneath them. These people have important things to do and don't like to waste time meandering or sightseeing. If you look closely at Powerful Choleric faces, you may see a scowl. Not because they are angry, although they may be, but because they are very intense people. Whatever Powerful Cholerics do, they do with complete determination. As they walk they will be thinking about their current project and what goals they have to attain.

At intimate social gatherings, you can recognize Powerful Cholerics as those who arrive late and leave early. They always have a very full schedule, and in order to get everything done, they sandwich social events between the important things. You may notice the Powerful Cholerics leave the room several times to make phone calls. If possible, they carry a cellular phone and may make a corner behind a potted palm into a temporary office.

When you talk with Powerful Cholerics you will find they have no respect of your "space." They move in very close to you and be totally unaware of how uncomfortable you may be. You back up a step or two, and unconsciously they move forward. If you find yourself talking to someone and you are backed against a wall, wishing you could get away, you are probably being pressured by a Powerful Choleric.

Strong Gestures

You will frequently see Powerful Cholerics pointing their index finger for emphasis. It's a part of their strong presence. In some cases, if they are really worked up, both the right and the left index finger may be pointing at the same time. We call these "Double-Fingered Cholerics." In some cases, they may even pound on desks or other nearby surfaces to be sure you get the picture. These gestures are sure giveaways for the Powerful Choleric person.

Their clothing is less distinct than Popular Sanguines' or Perfect Melancholies', but there are still several features you can watch for in the Powerful Choleric. A businessman may or may not adhere to the typical "power" dressing techniques, but he will probably have functional shoes. Both Powerful Choleric men and women choose footwear for its function rather than its beauty. The men will tend to shy away from those delicate leather Italian loafers and be more attracted to a sturdy American-made wingtip or tasseled loafer. Women will avoid spike-heeled pointy-toed shoes that pinch their feet. If a Powerful Choleric woman wears heels at all, they will be low, wide heels that provide good support and balance. She can't walk at the standard powerful pace in fragile little shoes.

Male or female, Powerful Cholerics will stay away from fashion trends and opt instead for good basic pieces that will last from year to year. They typically don't like to shop as they see the activity as a waste of productive time. Therefore, clothing that is versatile and lasting will be their first choice. They will avoid fussy touches, a style more obvious in a woman's dress than a man's. The Powerful Choleric woman will be uncomfortable in lace, ruffles, and bows. She keeps her jewelry to a minimum of basic pieces, and she'll find scarves to be frustrating and in the way. Florence can't stand scarves around her neck; she feels as if she's wrapped up in bandages.

You may need to spend a little more time getting to know Powerful Choleric people in order to determine their personality style because they don't have the obvious clothing traits. But, that in itself is a way to identify them. By process of elimination you can tell they are not Popular Sanguines if they do not have flashy clothing and that they are not Perfect Melancholies if the details of their clothes and appearance are not meticulously put together. If they are dressed in good basic clothes *and* exhibit an intensity, revealed through their fast-paced, heavy-footed walk, and they point their fingers as they talk, you probably have found Powerful Cholerics.

No Frills at Work

Powerful Cholerics have a "no frills" approach to their work environment. Their time is so consumed with the tasks at hand that they don't bother to even notice if there are pictures on the wall or if the furniture matches. Powerful Cholerics would rather use old desks that work, even if they are unattractive, than new ones that lack their favorite features.

When we moved into new, bigger office facilities, we wanted to get Florence some matching furniture pieces for her office. She had never really had an office of her own before because Fred had felt that when she was away on the road so much she didn't need to tie up expensive space that could be rented to someone else. The area she did have was filled with leftover mismatched pieces.

As a Popular Sanguine, Florence was excited about choosing just the right pieces and made quite a production out of the whole process, visiting many furniture stores. Fred, a Powerful Choleric combined with Perfect Melancholy, went shopping with her even though he didn't think he needed anything new for himself.

Fred's office furniture consisted of an old, dark, heavy wood desk with tarnished brass handles. Fred likes to have a glass top on his desk so he can press firmly when he writes and still not damage the surface, but some time ago the glass had been broken. One of the employees mentioned a friend who owned a glass shop. This friend was willing to cut the glass for Fred's desk and give it to him free if he would take some used green window glass. This gift appealed to Fred's practical nature.

For his files, Fred had several mismatched two-drawer file cabinets. They were of varying heights and wood grains and one drawer could only be opened halfway or the entire thing would fall at your feet. These uneven file cabinets were lined up against one wall.

Next to his desk he had an inexpensive typewriter stand where he kept the phone and his schedule book. The stand had chrome legs and a plastic laminate fake oak surface. When guests came to visit, they sat in brown vinyl discount store chairs.

Fred was perfectly happy there in familiar, comfortable, and practical surroundings. Once he was inside his office he was so consumed with his work that he didn't take time to worry about whether things matched or were in good repair.

However, when Fred went shopping with Florence, he, too, came back with new and attractive matching office furniture, even though he didn't really think he needed it and was afraid it was too big an expenditure. Now and then he still complains about his current furniture because it doesn't have all the amenities he had created for himself with his previous mishmash of pieces, and he misses his big old broken chair. Remember the Powerful Choleric is more interested in function than fluff and the Perfect Melancholy is thrifty, sometimes perceived as cheap. A person with both personalities feels there's no point in spending money for new items if the old ones are still functional.

Strong Ads for Powerful Cholerics

Popular Sanguines look for fun and popularity, but Powerful Cholerics are after power and control. Naturally, ads for big-ticket items that move or have motors (like cars, trucks, and boats) or that facilitate active sports (skiing, racing, or shooting) are often geared toward the Powerful Choleric who usually controls the family spending anyway.

Ads that appeal to Powerful Cholerics use powerful words, often sports or engine metaphors for things that have nothing to do with sports or machines. An ad for investment opportunities that would help jump start the economy as well as beat competitors at their own game is nearly guaranteed to appeal to Powerful Cholerics.

Powerful Choleric ads have bigger and more words in them—often repeated more than once. Words like *grand, powerful, greatest, best,* or *biggest* are tip-offs to Powerful Choleric ad appeal. So are big, bold letters and hard-hitting video images. No soft colors or flimsy, romantic lighting for Powerful Cholerics.

Powerful Cholerics want action and power even in their vacations (if they take them). Vacation spots that promise competitive sports activities or the possibility of doing some business while playing most appeal to them. Popular Sanguines want action too, but they want fun action. They do not want to know that they could do business while on vacation.

The Visible Pieces

While we are catching our breath from the fun of the Popular Sanguine and the excitement of the Powerful Choleric, let's review the visible pieces. We can see Popular Sanguines are colorful, talkative people. We can practice recognizing their personality even in advertising. And we can learn to appeal to them with the offer of fun and popularity.

We know that Perfect Melancholies are neat, meticulous, and analytical. They are attracted to ads that show mechanical items and organizational tools that give statistics, values, and charts. We can reach them by presenting our case meticulously and logically.

Powerful Cholerics exhibit strength and power in words and action. They are attracted to things and situations they can control. And we can reach them with the offer of challenging opportunities.

So whether we are planning to see, to sell, or simply to make our workday life run smoother, we can do it by recognizing the pieces of the Personality Puzzle.

CHAPTER 5

Peaceful Phlegmatics:
The Blue Sky in Your Puzzle

Spotting the Peaceful Phlegmatic visually is perhaps the hardest. They are middle-of-the-road people and don't exhibit obvious traits. Vice President Dan Quayle has been labeled "an amiable golfer," "a genial fellow," "an all-round nice guy"—all pleasant Peaceful Phlegmatic assets. His supposed weaknesses have been touted by comedians who have made him out to be a Ken doll spouting the latest blonde jokes. Actually, Quayle has grown into his position. He has been willing to take instruction from veteran politicians, to study and gain knowledge on government, and to master the complex details of military procurement and arms control—all this without making any noise about it.

When the *Washington Post* did a series of investigative reports on Dan Quayle (January 1992), they couldn't come up with anything reprehensible, try as we could assume they did. They complimented his quiet ability, his tact in handling difficult situations, and his wisdom in accepting advice from his wife—who appears to be an obvious Powerful Choleric in our estimation.

The *Los Angeles Times* (9 Jan. 1992) said that Quayle "lacks the indefinable sense of authority" perhaps due to his relative youth and that his "image has been persistently unconvincing." However, they agree that he has no obvious faults and that if he became president "the immediate trappings of the office and the solemnity of the occasion would envelop the man with the necessary aura."

Dan Quayle fits the Peaceful Phlegmatic image. Even though the Peaceful Phlegmatic is not an obvious personality visually, below are some specifics that will help give you clues in identifying them.

Easy Does It

As the blue-sky pieces of the Personality Puzzle, Peaceful Phlegmatics make up the background of life and therefore are the most difficult to identify through obvious and noticeable traits. This is the best way to identify the Peaceful Phlegmatic; they aren't any of the other personalities. Peaceful Phlegmatics have no obvious faults, and they can be happy anywhere.

As you might guess, their clothing choices are most likely to be as casual as the situation will allow. Jeans and sweatshirts are a Peaceful Phlegmatic favorite.

Peaceful Phlegmatics like to be in the background and don't want to attract a lot of attention to themselves. They'll avoid the flashy colors of the Popular Sanguine and opt instead for the more muted natural colors. In fact, the entire natural look works very well for Peaceful Phlegmatics since wrinkles don't bother them and natural fibers wrinkle easily. They choose loose-fitting clothes. Whether or not the pieces truly go together is of little concern. They will often simply pick whatever is on the top of the pile.

Peaceful Phlegmatics are the exact opposite of Powerful Cholerics. This is carried through into their walking styles. While Powerful Cholerics walk with purpose and a heavy foot, Peaceful Phlegmatics flow. They are light-footed and can pass by without disturbing a soul. Their body movements seem almost fluid as they saunter by hoping to go unnoticed.

Powerful Cholerics have trouble resting, but rest is a favorite pastime of Peaceful Phlegmatics. They are good workers. But, once the work is done, they will take their deserved rest rather than hunt for another project. At social events they are happy to socialize—if those who wish to talk to them come to where they are seated. They have a unique ability to quickly size up the furniture and select the most comfortable seat. Once that's done, they may camp there for the entire evening. In locating the Peaceful Phlegmatic, look for the person who is standing quietly on the edge of the action leaning against a wall or door frame or relaxing on a sofa.

Low-Key Speech

When you talk to Peaceful Phlegmatics, their speech will have a tranquilizing pace that calms you down as they talk. The Peaceful Phlegmatics will speak only when they really feel someone cares to hear them. They never interrupt, and they become wonderful listeners for Popular Sanguines looking for an audience. Rather than the laugh-a-minute approach of Popular Sanguine, Peaceful Phlegmatic will slide in some subtle humor, usually on the dry or witty side.

Peaceful Workplace

In the workplace, Peaceful Phlegmatics are happy just about anywhere. Our Peaceful Phlegmatic, Melissa, worked for us for a year and a half before going away to college. During that time she never had a desk of her own. She kept her file folder in someone else's desk. Since she worked in the afternoons and some of our other staff worked in the mornings, Melissa used whichever desk was available. She never complained or used her lack of space as an excuse. She just moved her folder from place to place.

When the Peaceful Phlegmatic does have a workspace, it is usually basically neat, although it may be littered with various half-finished projects. Peaceful Phlegmatics don't like conflict. If they run into a snag while they are working on a project, they will find it easier to set the project aside for another day than to push for resolution of the complication. They have a low motivation level and can postpone completion with no sense of guilt.

Peaceful Phlegmatics like to keep everything on their desk within easy reach. You may often see them scooting their desk chair across the floor to get a needed item rather than getting off their seat and walking to find it.

Blend In

Peaceful Phlegmatics are always the most difficult to recognize in person because of their balance, calm demeanor, and lack of extremes. Popular Sanguines make grand entrances and entertain people; Powerful Cholerics walk with confidence and speak with authority; perfectly put together Perfect Melancholies quietly take in the mood of the moment. Peaceful Phlegmatics blend in with the group and silently suit the situation. They fit the verse, "laugh with those who laugh; weep with those who weep."

No Hurry

Jeff is one of two Peaceful Phlegmatics in our office. He has a gentle spirit, never complains, and prays for all the rest of us. He comes in on time, does his work quietly and efficiently, and has never yet shown any anger or temper. He works well with Powerful Choleric and Perfect Melancholy Fred who wants things done his way, perfectly. Jeff never bucks authority, tries his best to please, and maintains a submissive attitude. When Jeff returned from his Christmas vacation he surprised us all; he had grown a beard. There was no real enthusiasm from the office staff over this addition, and after a week or so Jeff decided he'd shave it off. Not wanting to move too fast or work at it too hard, Jeff shaved a little at a time. The first day he came in with an inch or two shaved in front of each ear. The next day, he had moved in toward his mouth but still sported a goatee and mustache. On the third day the goatee was missing, but he still had the mustache. We could hardly wait for the next morning. Sure enough the mustache was gone. When I mentioned the gradual disappearance of his facial hair, he replied "There was no hurry and I decided to do it in stages."

Ads That Say Easy Does It

Peaceful Phlegmatics aren't easy to caricature, nor are they easy targets for media and advertising. In general, ads that appeal to Peaceful Phlegmatics do not make any outrageous promises or grandiose guarantees. While the Perfect Melancholy may be put off by a guarantee because it seems to be statistically skewed, the Peaceful Phlegmatic won't like it simply because it is *so* enthusiastic and jarring.

Peaceful Phlegmatics do like ads that promise products or services that are easy to use, simple, and ordinary. No bright colors and flashing lights here. Hair color or makeup ads that promise you'll be able to accomplish a difference in mere minutes *and* look so natural that no one will know the look isn't really natural are likely to appeal to Peaceful Phlegmatic women.

If any clothing ad at all appealed to a Peaceful Phlegmatic man it would be one for casual, inexpensive, wear-it-anywhere sports clothes. Easy to wash, no ironing, and available by simply phoning in an order from a catalog would all be benefits.

In general, words like *gently, easy to use, peaceful, soothing, restful,* and the like appeal to Peaceful Phlegmatics. Travel ads that promise rest and relaxation also appeal.

Look for the ads that picture people sitting on the beach doing nothing. Find the ones that offer door-to-door service, preferably from house to airport to hotel with twenty-four hour room service. Those are ads with Peaceful Phlegmatic appeal. Basking in gentle breezes may seem boring to Popular Sanguines or useless to Powerful Cholerics. The difference between beach ads that feature Perfect Melancholies and Peaceful Phlegmatics lying in the sun is subtle. Perfect Melancholies might well be inclined to lie on the beach in order to regain peace of mind and new insight into life's challenges. Peaceful Phlegmatics simply want to lie on the beach and need no perceived benefit beyond that.

Seeing Is Believing

Practice the Personality Puzzle by observing people, by scrutinizing print and television ads, or by watching interactions in movies. You begin to be aware of the visible differences between individuals. Knowing the differences is the first step to fitting the people in your workday puzzle together.

As you've read through these pages, you've probably been fitting individuals you work with—and yourself—into categories, trying to see who fits most obviously where. This would be a good time to make a list of people you work with and write down which piece in the puzzle you think each is. Simply doing that exercise will make you more aware of your own particular players. It will also give you a baseline for fitting your players into the various pieces and seeing how they work together harmoniously —or don't—and how you can value each and every one of them—no matter who you are or who they are.

It's just as important to figure out which of the descriptions fits you best as to figure out what types other people are. Working together, of course, means interacting. Which personality type looks most like you?

Look around at your work environment. Is there a place for everything and everything in its place? Do you have stacks of projects out in plain sight? Have you refused to give up a comfortable old chair even though the upholstery is holier than a saint? Are you comfortable working just about anywhere?

What's hanging in your closet? Maybe more to the point, what always hangs in your closet because you won't willingly wear it? That khaki suit

your mother encouraged you to buy because it would look more professional while your teal and orange outfits are practically worn out? That
bright green print dress, just the right color to go with your eyes, that
makes you feel like a walking billboard? Those new "retro" ties with big
prints and loud colors that your wife bought you for Christmas? Or don't
you know what's in your closet? Peaceful Phlegmatics wouldn't.

One of the "hidden" benefits of figuring out how your friends and
coworkers fit into the Personality Puzzle is that you get to know a lot more
about yourself. Once you've pegged yourself, you'll get a lot more out of
the rest of this book. Knowing yourself and others means working successfully with people you've been knocking heads with for years. Whole
new avenues of creative accomplishments and harmonious undertakings
are opening up to you.

PART TWO

The Various Pieces of the Puzzle

How to Understand the Personalities in Your Workplace

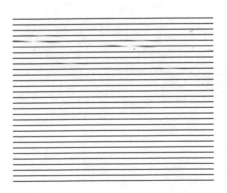

CHAPTER 6

Putting the Various Pieces Together

Once you have seen the personalities in your life you will never look at people the same way again. You can now begin to put this new knowledge to work for you! Each personality type has specific, different, and natural appearances and mannerisms. Each also has some basic behavior patterns that go hand in hand with the visual pieces of the puzzle. In this section on the various pieces of the puzzle, we look at the strengths and weaknesses of each personality profile.

As you learn to understand the people in your own life, this section will help you confirm the personality placement of those people. You will have a more realistic idea of what to expect from each person in your workplace. Suddenly, a more appropriate distribution of tasks and responsibilities will appear. If you are a manager, you'll be able to assign work more effectively. If you are a "worker bee," you'll be able to use your newfound knowledge to interact more effectively with colleagues up and down the corporate chart. No matter what kind of paid or volunteer work you do, fitting those you associate with into the Personality Puzzle will help *all* of you get along better and achieve better results.

Without these pieces in the puzzle, we tend to expect each person to react the same way to a given situation. We often assume everyone will see things the way we do. These kinds of expectations set us up for, at best, disappointment and delays and, at worst, failure and hurt.

"If possible, so far as it depends on you, be at peace with all men" (Rom. 12:18 NAS). This scripture implies that we will not be at peace with everyone, but it does tell us that it is up to us to try. With an understanding of the various personalities in your workplace, you will have much better chances of "being at peace" with those who cross your path on a regular basis.

Think of those you work with. You've placed many of them into the puzzle as you looked at the *visual* pieces. As you read about the *various* pieces, you can firmly place each person into the right part of the puzzle.

Marita has a super Powerful Choleric business associate. Cynthia replaced a sweet little Peaceful Phlegmatic southern belle. Obviously they communicate in very different styles. The Peaceful Phlegmatic spoke slowly and thought about things before making decisions. She always asked how business was and freely offered the weather report for her part of the country. When Cynthia came on board, Marita thought Cynthia didn't like her. Their phone calls were brief and to the point. Cynthia didn't give or request weather reports; her responses came quickly and needed no deliberation. When Marita and Cynthia finally met at an industry convention, Cynthia's opening comment was, "So, tell me what it is you really do for us." Marita, who lives on the praises of her clients, thought that Cynthia wasn't happy with the service she had been providing and began somewhat defensively. Cynthia jumped in and assured Marita that she was pleased with the work but as the new player on the team she just didn't understand the whole arrangement.

As they talked face to face over lunch, Marita could clearly place Cynthia in the Powerful Choleric part of the puzzle. What she had interpreted as dissatisfaction was simply the Powerful Choleric way of doing business. Once Marita understood Cynthia's personality, she could accept the brusque treatment as simply a matter-of-fact way of dealing with life rather than as a personal issue. Marita knows not to bother Cynthia with fluffy conversation, and Cynthia appreciates Marita's efficiency.

Now when they have phone conversations, Marita knows not to waste time chitchatting. The needs are covered and then they are both back to business with a minimal interruption of the work flow. Every few months, Cynthia assures Marita that she is satisfied and the relationship functions like a well-oiled machine.

At a recent convention Marita asked Cynthia, "Do we need to talk?" Cynthia answered, "No. I'm fine. Are you?" Marita agreed that everything was functioning well, and they both went their own way to deal with those problem-prone people who needed attention!

When we understand the *various* pieces of the puzzle, we can place the personalities in our workplace where they belong. No more square pegs in round holes.

When Rod was in graduate school one of his professors, who was also the head of the department, was an obvious Popular Sanguine. At the beginning of every class, she promptly kicked off her shoes. During the hour she frequently got off on tangents. At the end of the class she would remark at how quickly the time had gone. As she dismissed the class, she'd shrug and say, "Oh, I never include all that I intend to, but we have such fun!" As long as she'd had fun she seemed quite pleased with herself whether or not she'd covered the material. Her free spirit and her need for fun were sure giveaways to her true personality.

Since Rod understood these concepts well, he was able to slant his projects and personal contacts to her liking. In a major report, Rod added many pictures and stories to appeal to her Popular Sanguine nature rather than the charts and statistics that would have been his Perfect Melancholy tendency. Of course his project got a perfect score, and, for weeks, every time he saw that professor she commented on how wonderful his project was. Throughout his program she made exceptions for Rod and recommended him for additional studies and honors work.

While some of his colleagues found her changeable standards and flexible style to be frustrating, Rod understood her and was able to relate to her in a way that she easily responded to, even though she didn't know what he was doing. We will always get along better when we deal into the other person's personality and not out of our own.

As you read the following section, you will gain an even clearer picture of how your puzzle fits together. If you are a manager, you will be better equipped to place different personalities into positions where they will function at their best. If you are struggling to get along with a boss, you will be able to understand his or her viewpoint and appeal to his or her personality needs. If the man at the next desk is driving you crazy, you will realize that his behaviors are not aimed at bothering you but rather are simply an outflowing of who he is. If you deal with clients, you can approach each one with a style that will relate to them the best. Do unto them as they would want you to do.

Whatever the picture is in your place of business, understanding how all the personalities fit into the puzzle will make your life more pleasant and may even make a game out of your workplace!

CHAPTER 7

Popular Sanguine:
Are We Having Fun Yet?

Strengths	*Weaknesses*
■ loves people	■ motivated by emotions
■ makes friends quickly	■ dislikes schedules
■ exciting	■ can't say "No"
■ finds jobs easily	■ makes excuses
■ good sense of humor	■ gets bored easily
■ charms others to work	■ loses track of time
■ creative and colorful	■ takes on too much
■ thrives on activity	■ easily distracted
■ natural sales ability	■ lacks focus
■ engaging storyteller	■ talks too much

In piecing together the personalities in your workplace it is important to realize that all the individuals are born with a built-in desire. Left to their own, this basic desire forms their behavior pattern. If there were no bosses, deadlines, or rules these basic desires would control their standard mode of operation. If there is no childhood trauma, abuse, or rejection, we will all have the same personality pattern at age eighty that we had at eight.

Popular Sanguine's basic desire is to have fun! More than anything else the Popular Sanguine likes to have a good time and be the life of the party, hence the descriptive heading of *popular*. The bumper sticker "Are we having fun yet?" accurately asks the Popular Sanguine's main question of life.

A Popular Sanguine volunteered to usher at church because he thought it would be fun to go up and down the aisles and see who was there. This young man had apparently never ushered. While he was spontaneous and obviously enjoyed the attention, he was not careful to observe the order of passing the offering bags—some rows had two bags converging in the middle while other rows were bypassed altogether!

Thrives on Activity

Popular Sanguines prefer to totally avoid work because work is seldom fun. Since that is unrealistic, they are most successful in jobs that allow them flexibility and contact with people. Having fun typically involves people and Popular Sanguine loves a crowd.

Flexibility is important because Popular Sanguines tend to operate from their feelings rather than from their heads. The calendar may indicate it's time to get to work on a project or go to a specific place. But if Popular Sanguines don't feel like doing that job, or are motivated by a new and different project, they can easily postpone the important task without guilt.

Flexibility is also important because Popular Sanguines often lose all track of time. They may be at an event that is so much fun that they never get back to the office that day. Joel was frequently missing from the office. He worked in the video unit of the police department. As a part of his loose job description he was responsible for researching and acquiring the needed video equipment. This meant he had to visit the various supply houses in town on a regular basis. He became good friends with everyone at each source. If a cable was needed or a deck had to be repaired, Joel was the one to take care of it. He was often gone for hours even though the shop may have been just a few blocks away. Once on site, Joel visited with everyone. They showed him all the latest pieces and he played with all the toys.

Since Joel was so well-loved, he frequently was able to finagle freebies from their suppliers. He knew all the "on air" personalities and local dignitaries. As a favor to Joel they frequently donated both time and money to the department's projects. While it might appear that Joel was neglectful of his duties, his Popular Sanguine personality worked in both his personal favor and that of the entire department.

A doctor Florence went to had a delightful Popular Sanguine nurse who made all the patients feel glad that they had come, even when they came in sick. One day the mood changed. The office seemed dull and gloomy. At the desk was a sullen woman working over the books. She barely looked up as she asked the patients' names and then told each one firmly to sit down and wait.

Florence waited her turn. But when she saw the doctor, she asked what had happened to the other nurse. He explained that he fired her because she could never get the books to balance.

Florence took the opportunity to give him a quick lecture on the Personality Puzzle, explaining that he should not have expected the first nurse to do the book work. Her strength was in keeping the patients happy and in making sickness bearable.

He admitted that everyone missed her and that the new woman, who could add and subtract, basically disliked people. During the discussion, he decided to get a part-time Popular Sanguine to work during office hours and to use the Perfect Melancholy to keep the books and billing in order.

He reported his success during Florence's next visit. When she was not bothered by patients, the Perfect Melancholy got her work done in fewer hours. The Popular Sanguine was happy to work only when the office was open and there was activity and people to talk with. Amazingly enough, this well-balanced flexible arrangement did not cost him any more because both were working part-time. And his patients were happy.

Marita's office has four Popular Sanguines, and by their own admission, "Boy, do we have fun!" As they deal by telephone with television and radio stations across the country, the person on the other end of the line will often say, "You all sound like you are having too much fun there." They are. Fridays often turn into pizza day and someone's birthday offers another good excuse for a party. Marita's office has become such a fun place to work that the employees look forward to coming to work and are shocked when it's "time to go home already." They have a large sign on the wall that says, "Reality is only for those who lack imagination." They firmly believe that a little denial, now and then, is good for everyone.

Part of what makes their job fun is the flexibility. Popular Sanguines, who are inherently averse to schedules, thrive on spontaneous activity. Marita's staff has a general time they are supposed to arrive at work and a time they leave. They arrive at different hours, depending on the schedule and the day. If someone needs to leave early, she just comes in earlier. Marita has tried to make up schedules and insist that everyone get in on time, but all that structure seemed to do was ruin the mood and detract from their creativity. And it didn't make anybody more efficient.

They don't take breaks once they do arrive. They eat at their desks, and they often work right through lunch. However, if someone has a problem, they are quick to console one another, hug, weep, wail, and pray. The first few minutes of the day are frequently spent catching up on the personal details of each other's lives.

Engaging Storyteller

Popular Sanguines have a natural ability to make even the simplest of happenings funny. They often add colorful details to a story. When they report on an adventure, they will take twice as long to tell it as the others would. People who were there often won't even recognize the story as the same event. They are willing to reveal someone's personal secret if it makes the story better. They often say, "I shouldn't tell you this, but . . ." immediately drawing in an attentive audience.

Once in a while the Popular Sanguines in Marita's office get so carried away with their stories, she has to snap them back to the work awaiting them. She claps her hands or simply hollers, "Back to work." In a matter of moments, everyone is back at work.

Popular Sanguines need other people around them to test out ideas and compliment their projects. When we were preparing to move into new office space, we had the opportunity to design our suites however we wanted. Fred thought he was doing them all a favor by planning separate offices for each of the staff. When the chatty Popular Sanguines heard of the plans they quickly changed them. They couldn't bear the thought of being separated in little rooms. They said they needed to be together because they feed on each other's hyperactivity. Now when Perfect Melancholy Fred is in the office, he closes the door between his part of the office and theirs because of the noise. One day he said, "The only mistake I made in designing these offices is I should have made thicker walls."

Can't Say "No"

With all that activity, you might wonder how Popular Sanguines ever get anything done. Sometimes they wonder too! It is important to Popular Sanguines to have friends and for everyone to like them. Therefore they tend to take on too many projects at one time. They have a tough time saying "no" and find themselves drowning in so many different projects they are afraid they'll never be able to pull them all off. But with a knack that seems to be unique to the Popular Sanguine, somehow everything always comes out right.

Howard is a pastor and his Popular Sanguine personality is appealing in the pulpit, but like most Popular Sanguines, Howard keeps getting distracted by other wonderful offers that come his way that have nothing to do with the church. Popular Sanguines have an air about them that gives others the feeling they can do anything, and job opportunities have a way of landing in their laps. In the two years since Howard started with the church, he has had numerous other projects in addition to his pastoral duties. A friend of his worked on bankrupt building projects, and Howard helped him on some of the marketing that needed to be done. Howard has also been a literary agent, helping his friends get their manuscripts published. He has bought, fixed up, and sold used cars. His current project is speaking at assemblies in the public high schools. Despite Howard's diverse activities, his enthusiasm has held the church together. People want to come to see what Howard is up to this week.

Popular Sanguines are much like cats. They seem to have nine lives, and they always land on their feet. If you struggle with Popular Sanguines at work, you may have already noticed that they get away with things others would have been fired for long ago. Their built-in charm and positive attitude will get them through the worst of times. If you have Popular Sanguine employees who are constantly living on the edge, don't worry. They may be a little late, so give them a deadline that is slightly ahead of the real need. They may be full of excuses, but if they get the project done, they'll expect praise. The more praise they get, the better they'll do next time. If they don't get it done, you can appeal to their sense of wanting to be liked to motivate them for next time. They usually pull through with flying colors and sometimes even win praise for work someone else has done, which is something to watch out for or even to use to your advantage. If you work for a Popular Sanguine, you can often get the boss to agree to let you try something new if you can show how it will win him or her praise.

Lacks Focus

Samantha is a Popular Sanguine artist. Like Howard, she's had no trouble finding jobs, and like many other Popular Sanguines, Samantha has had trouble focusing on what she wants to do with her life. While Popular Sanguines have so much energy that they often make people tired just watching them and their enthusiasm pulls them out of most problems, they are easily distracted, undisciplined, and lack follow-through. Samantha is very talented and, unlike a Perfect Melancholy artist who might take years to produce a perfect painting, she could probably make a living with her quick style that enables her to whip up a project in a single evening. Unfortunately for Samantha, she has a short interest span and after she completes a painting she often changes her mind. She then paints over the previous night's work and comes up with a totally different look.

Samantha started a jewelry company and made one-of-a-kind artsy pins and earrings. She had cute business cards made up and sold a few orders to Nieman-Marcus. But once she'd done that, she became bored and didn't make as much money as she'd hoped. She still has quite a bit of stock left, but now she's selling cars, as she did a few years earlier. Samantha has also been a high school art teacher and a career counselor, has sold diet plans, and has worked in retail sales.

With her Popular Sanguine personality, Samantha is able to find a new job fast. Unfortunately, none of them turn out to be the job she'd hoped to find and she moves on to the next one, typically within a few months. The negative in this shifting of Popular Sanguines' interests is that they find themselves mid-life with no real career, a long, varied resume, and no security.

All of Samantha's jobs have two ingredients in common. They all involve working with people and in one way or another are a form of sales.

You may be a Popular Sanguine or find yourself counseling one about a career. It's important for Popular Sanguines to look for flexibility and variety. Finding a job that provides something different every day can help Popular Sanguines stick to one job long enough to make a career. Popular Sanguines' lack of focus in one setting can be a benefit in a job requiring constantly shifting focus, especially in response to new opportunities.

Natural Sales Ability

Popular Sanguines are natural born salespeople. Sales allows them flexibility and an opportunity to be with people. They make friends quickly, and they have an innate sense of innocence. With that combination, they appear to sincerely have your best interests at heart.

One morning in a hotel coffee shop, Fred and Florence became increasingly aware that the handsome young man at the next table was a Popular Sanguine. He was entertaining his friend with a review of the previous night's party. When he noticed they were listening, he pulled his chair over closer and added them to his audience. He dramatized the events of the previous evening. He had put on a dance in a hotel for 1500 people, but he had no idea if he had made or lost money. "The one with the money left," he explained. In hilarious fashion, he then shared that he was an aerobics instructor who also sells dance supplies and leotards. "I can sell the ladies anything as long as I tell them it will enhance their beauty." When Fred asked him how business was going, he replied, "I don't think I'm making much, but I'm not sure. I just take out what I need and hope there's something left over."

Fred was appalled at his total lack of concern over money and gave him a few words of Perfect Melancholy advice.

When the young man rose to leave, he gave us his name and then introduced his buddy in Popular Sanguine fashion, "This is my friend. He is a poor imitation of me."

The friend nodded in agreement and off they went. Only a Popular Sanguine could have the charm and magnetism to get away with such a statement and still keep his friend.

Popular Sanguines find it easy to live on their personality and carry their ability to charm others to an extreme. They learn early in life that if they can make others have fun and feel good about themselves they can rise to the top. Unfortunately, this sometimes backfires, especially in politics.

Consider a man who was elected mayor of a large city. He was a born politician with movie-star looks and a magnetic personality to go with them. He amassed support from an unusual coalition of voters from disparate interest groups in his city.

The problem for magnetic Popular Sanguine politicians is that charming people is so easy that conning them is often the next step. They don't mean to be crooked, but it's too easy not to take what's offered. That's what happened to this particular mayor. He was accused of using his office to extract favors and bribes. However, even after he was accused and didn't run for reelection, he found himself with many supporters.

Popular Sanguines' creativity and natural people skills will make them assets to any business. Keep them out front with the people, and give them flexibility and a lot of variety. Don't expect Popular Sanguines to be detail conscious, schedule oriented, or perfectionistic. In the right place, Popular Sanguines are the best of both popularity and productivity.

CHAPTER 8

Perfect Melancholy: Are Things Perfect Yet?

Strengths

- works well alone
- planner
- good with numbers
- likes charts and graphs
- organized
- appreciates quiet
- accurate
- analytical
- fair
- loves beauty

Weaknesses

- easily depressed
- lacks spontaneity
- naively idealistic
- thrifty to extremes
- doesn't do well under pressure
- excessively perfectionistic
- needs plenty of time
- hard to please

Perfect Melancholies' basic desire is for—you guessed it—perfection. Their goal is to have all of life in order. The Perfect Melancholy creed is "If it is worth doing, it is worth doing right!"

Melancholy by its dictionary definition is synonymous with depth, depression, or blackness. The weather may be melancholy or a person may be described as being in a melancholy mood. While not all Perfect Melancholies are depressed—and in fact they can be very cheerful—when your goal in life is to achieve perfection, you are bound to be disappointed. When was the last time you had a perfect hour, let alone day, week, or month? Perfection is elusive, and while one area of our lives may reach perfection the others are possibly in ruin from neglect.

Yet, despite its unattainability, deep down inside Perfect Melancholies still long for perfection. In total contrast to Popular Sanguines, who need people, Perfect Melancholies generally prefer to work alone. People are the ones who mess things up. This doesn't mean Perfect Melancholies are recluses, although the extreme Perfect Melancholy may be. It simply means that they would appreciate a private workspace without noise or interruption.

Needs Plenty of Time

Where Popular Sanguines may view a deadline as the time to get started on a project, Perfect Melancholies don't do well under pressure. They will do best if they are informed of a deadline well in advance. They need the time to get the job done and have time to redo it if it is not perfect.

Buck's family owns a manufacturing company that makes plastic sleeving for film. Among his many management duties is producing their catalog. While Buck has most of the materials and equipment he needs to produce the catalog at the office, he prefers to do it at home. He's happy spending days home alone in front of the computer and eventually he will produce a perfect product.

One night during this catalog process, Buck's Popular Sanguine wife, Jerece, wanted to see a movie. When she asked him about going out, he said he couldn't spare the time because he had to get a project done. Later Jerece found out the project wasn't due for a month. But like a true Perfect Melancholy, Buck had set deadlines for himself to be sure that everything was completed well ahead of schedule with enough time to allow for problems. He couldn't take time off for fun because it would have thrown off his schedule.

Perfect Melancholies who are young enough to have caught the computer bug love all the intricacies of computers and the data they can store. They can produce perfect-looking letters, forms, and projects. No more erasing, whiting out mistakes, or retyping. These people devour computer magazines and get almost excited over each new computer gadget.

Excessively Perfectionistic

Remember Popular Sanguine Pastor Howard? Perfect Melancholy Buck started attending Howard's church. Buck asked Howard for a "statement of faith." Knowing what you know about the Popular Sanguine, do you suppose Howard had a "statement of faith"? Of course he didn't, but he is a quick thinker. He handed Buck a large manual from denominational headquarters and told him the first forty pages would cover it. Howard was sure that no one cared enough about a statement of faith to read forty pages, but Howard was thinking as a Popular Sanguine.

Buck took the manual home to read. The following week he returned the manual. And he presented Howard with forty nice clean laser printed pages. Buck had scanned the forty pages into his computer, made grammatical and spelling corrections, and given Howard a clean *and* correct copy for the next person who asked for a statement of faith.

The Perfect Melancholy's need for perfection goes beyond efficiency or looking pretty. It is an almost uncontrollable need to fix things. Howard didn't ask Buck to correct the manual. He didn't even know it had mistakes because he'd never read it himself. But it wasn't perfect and without thinking about it, Buck corrected it on his own. Buck assumed that anyone seeing imperfections would want them corrected. How surprised the denominational president was when he received the pages with the changes. The statement of faith had been available for years and this was the first time anyone had noticed the errors. Naturally, Howard happily took the credit for the corrections.

Loves Beauty

We read a story in *Connoisseur* magazine (Sept. 1991) about a man named Rudolf Karl Staab, a German who was captivated by the Andalusian hills near Granada in Spain, and who seems to be a Perfect Melancholy. He had deep feelings for nature and found a magnificent setting on an imposing hill spotted with large rocks and olive groves. His creative mind pictured a luxury hotel carefully placed among the rock out-croppings, not disturbing even one of the olive trees. Improbable as it seemed to build a hotel in the hills forty-five miles away from the nearest city, Staab determined he could design the perfect hotel. And he has.

La Bobadilla has thirty-five exquisite rooms and suites with sunken tubs, private patios, hand-carved doors, and exceptional wrought-iron work. The construction and management of the hotel has become an obsession for Staab as he works night and day overseeing every detail. He has been given the title "El Perfeccionista," the perfectionist.

Connoisseur calls La Bobadilla "the finest hotel in all of Spain," and affirms that it "was designed in perfect harmony with the land, following Staab's original vision."

Accurate

Sometimes you can recognize people's personality without even seeing them. Rahla wrote us the following example:

> Since learning about the four personality types I have had fun wher-
> ever I am by observing the different temperaments in action. A recent
> event occurred during a flight on which I was returning home from the
> CLASS seminar in California.
>
> Shortly after takeoff the pilot welcomed us aboard and began to
> give a detailed description of the flight path. As I listened to the exact-
> ness of his description I immediately identified him as a Perfect Mel-
> ancholy. Although I was only hearing his voice, in my mind he could
> be standing at a flip-chart with pointer in hand defining our flight like
> a general briefing his troops on the next military campaign.
>
> In case any passengers had missed his initial commentary, this
> pilot continued to give updated information on specific geographic
> locations every fifteen to twenty minutes on a two-and-a-half-hour
> flight! This new data would include what we were currently flying
> over, what we could see from each side of the aircraft and a review of
> our flight path from that point measured in angles and degrees.
>
> . . . I marveled that I was observing a firsthand object lesson on a
> classic personality type immediately after the seminar. I thought of
> other flights I had been on and projected how the other three person-
> alities would relate to their passengers. A Popular Sanguine pilot
> would welcome everyone enthusiastically and on extremely long
> flights might even come out to personally greet them. Most of the
> flights I have been on must have had Powerful Choleric pilots—the
> requisite announcements were made after takeoff and before landing,
> but were concise and somewhat curt as if this were an intrusion into
> the business at hand. The Peaceful Phlegmatic pilot's voice would
> probably be the most comforting and soothing to those nervous or
> "first-time-flying" passengers.
>
> When this particular flight landed, as customarily happens the pas-
> sengers crowded into the aisle to try to deplane quickly. However, we

were held in this rather uncomfortable position at least five minutes while the stewardess read every conceivable connecting flight destination and its departing gate number. The entire flight crew was apparently Perfect Melancholy! As I exited the plane I thanked the pilot for being so informative and his face literally lit up, most likely at being appreciated for his helpful travelogue!

This ability to do things with complete accuracy is especially helpful in professions dealing with numbers, in manufacturing, and in most medical or dental fields.

When Florence went to visit her dentist to have some major work done, he was quite enthused because her teeth had several different shades in what he called stripes. This problem presented him with such an exciting challenge that he brought in a specialist. Together they made the needed crowns with the exact shading of her natural teeth. The results were "perfect." If you need to have your teeth worked on or your heart fixed, a Perfect Melancholy will be the one for the job.

Likes Charts and Graphs

Perfect Melancholies like analytical work and keep life in order through the use of charts and graphs. Karen, our Business Manager/Administrator, loves the challenge of selecting new equipment or computer programs. She checks with friends, talks to consultants, and calls salespeople. She compiles all the information into a chart or list and then draws a conclusion about which option will be the best for our long-term needs. While this approach may take longer, it often proves to be more effective in the long run. In contrast, Popular Sanguines likely choose what looks good or what their friends have. And Powerful Cholerics make instant, impulsive decisions and want them carried out that very afternoon.

Recently Karen had some concerns over mounting costs for upcoming seminars. On her own, she gathered up the figures for previous similar events and concluded that they had not been financial successes. Then she computed all the projected costs for the upcoming events and figured out how many people we needed at each one to break even. Karen printed out all her charts in a clean, professional-looking font and presented them to Fred. Once he saw the facts in plain black and white, or red as the case may be, he made the needed adjustments.

Analytical

Perfect Melancholies are naturally able to see problems and to invent complex, rule-oriented solutions. Bill is an eye surgeon and according to his Popular Sanguine wife, he is a Perfect Melancholy with a little bit of the Powerful Choleric. When Bill was a resident, his natural Perfect Melancholy tendencies observed several things in the department that were not "perfect." He made a list of everything that was wrong and unfair to the residents. Then Bill made a mistake that many Perfect Melancholies make. He thought that his superiors would be delighted with his observations and immediately fix the inequities. When he presented his list to his Powerful Choleric boss it was not received with great enthusiasm. With Perfect Melancholy idealism, Bill thought that his boss simply didn't understand the problems. So, to help him out Bill made a chart that outlined not only the problems but also offered detailed steps to straighten out the situation, with a complete plan for implementation.

Unfortunately Bill didn't understand the basic personality concepts so he didn't realize that his boss was a Powerful Choleric who didn't appreciate correction, especially unasked for and from a person of lower rank. If Bill had understood that not everyone wants to do things the way that he views as right and fair, he might have known to stop when his first suggestions were not well received. But Bill didn't know this, and he pushed for what he believed was right. One week before his wedding and well into his residency program, Bill was fired! The young couple had to cancel their honeymoon, get all their deposits back, and spend all the money they had saved for their honeymoon and for starting their new home to hire a lawyer. Bill did eventually get reinstated into the residency program. And today, if you need eye surgery, you can be sure that Bill will do a perfect job.

Naively Idealistic

Perfect Melancholies do tend to be idealistic and think, like Bill, that everyone will want to know the right way to do things. After all, "If it's worth doing, it's worth doing right." But that idealism can often bring about a downfall. An article in *Time* magazine ("Hail to the Ex-Chief," 11 Sept. 1989) that featured past President Jimmy Carter referred to what we're pretty sure is his Perfect Melancholy idealism. It highlighted his work for the homeless through Habitat for Humanity. The article concluded, "And you get the feeling that maybe this is what he thought the presidency would be like—all good works, no Ted Kennedys or Tip O'Neills or bureaucrats or special interests—when he set about from Plains many years ago, naively determined, against the odds, to make a difference." President Carter tried to make everything perfect and found that "perfection" isn't what government is all about.

Organized

While people skills may not be Perfect Melancholies' forte, they will be best in a position where things need to be done correctly. Gayle worked in a governmental agency and insisted that things be done her way. If she was typing a letter for someone, she rearranged things so that they were right! Some of the office staff found this to be very offensive since she reworked their letters without permission. Others appreciated her corrections. Her bosses always loved her efficiency. They knew that if they needed something done, Gayle would get it done correctly and on time. In fact, Gayle didn't need to be given deadlines or supervision. She was able to anticipate the needs and get them done before she was asked. With her Perfect Melancholy organizational ability, Gayle always knew where everything was and frequently bailed others out of their messes because she could put her hand on a file, form, or resource on a moment's notice. With a little appreciation on the part of her coworkers, Gayle thrived and the entire office functioned smoothly. If you put files back where they belonged and complimented her on being able to put her hand on what you needed, she'd be your friend for life. But if you looked through her files for the papers yourself, or if you forgot to put things back in the perfect spot, you would burn the bridge and incur her wrath, eliminating any hope of help in future. A sign on her desk summed up the Perfect Melancholy's work attitude toward those of less perfect personalities: "Poor planning on your part does not constitute an emergency on my part."

While not every Perfect Melancholy will have all of these characteristics, many of these stories may remind you of someone in your workplace. If you work with Perfect Melancholies, be grateful for their thorough thinking and ability to do things right. Be sure to compliment them for the talents they have. Let them work without interruption, and, if you're the boss, be sure to give them plenty of notice on project due dates. If for some reason you must get involved in their system, be sure to observe their guidelines and put things back where you found them or you may never get them again!

CHAPTER 9

Powerful Choleric: Am I in Charge Yet?

Strengths	Weaknesses
■ fearless activist	■ little need for friends
■ fixes problems	■ opinionated
■ decisive	■ overconfident
■ loves a challenge	■ can't relax
■ born leader	■ workaholic tendency
■ organizes quickly	■ expects complete devotion
■ production oriented	■ nervy
■ excels in crisis	■ usurps authority
■ exudes confidence	■ unemotional
■ usually right	■ arrogant
	■ manipulates others
	■ can't say "I'm sorry"
	■ fears losing control

As you have been piecing together the personalities in your workplace, you likely have several people who have some aspects of Popular Sanguines and/or Perfect Melancholies, but the pieces don't quite fit. They may be Powerful Cholerics, the corner pieces that hold everything and everyone together.

Powerful Cholerics have some similarities to Popular Sanguines. Both are extroverts, meaning that they enjoy being around people, although for different reasons. Popular Sanguines need people as audiences and as friends. In contrast, Powerful Cholerics don't need friends. In fact, they typically have very few. Their basic desire is for control. They are natural bosses and, in order for the Powerful Cholerics to be in control, they need people willing to be controlled. Powerful Cholerics have few fears and are confident being in front of a group of people. They are willing to take over any group or meeting even when they haven't been asked. If you want to know if the extroverts you work with are Powerful Cholerics or Popular Sanguines, ask yourself this question: Do they need people for production (the former) or socializing (the latter)?

Fixes Problems

Marita is a Popular Sanguine, and she is also half Powerful Choleric. She had a difficult time not getting up and fixing the things that weren't functioning right at her recent class reunion. When the blessing was offered before the food, no one was listening and it was all she could do to stay in her seat and not tap her glass with a spoon to quiet everyone down. Fortunately it was a brief blessing so she didn't have long to be impatient. However, once the program started, she couldn't contain her Powerful Choleric side any longer. The microphones were not working properly and she couldn't hear. She simply got up and found a hotel person who turned a knob and fixed the problem. Part of her Powerful Choleric personality just took control and fixed the problem.

Running things, righting wrongs, and fixing problems comes naturally to Powerful Cholerics, even if those in charge don't ask for help and sometimes don't even want it. Lack of appointment doesn't keep the Powerful Choleric from taking control.

Decisive

Powerful Cholerics share organizational skills with Perfect Melancholies. They both want things structured. But they don't agree on how that should be done. Perfect Melancholies like to write things down, make a chart, and think it over. Powerful Cholerics organize quickly in their heads and make instant pronouncements. By instinct, Powerful Cholerics are usually as right as Perfect Melancholies who spend time analyzing. The ability to "guess" correctly without study often irks Perfect Melancholies who think no one can possibly make correct decisions without a period of meditation. It just isn't fair that Powerful Cholerics thrive on crises that will throw

Perfect Melancholies into a depression or at least a minor decline. Powerful Cholerics like being at the helm in stormy weather while Perfect Melancholies try to stabilize life and get it perfect. They both want things done right and are production based. In contrast, Popular Sanguines and Peaceful Phlegmatics are socially based.

Usually Right

The slogan of every Powerful Choleric could be, "I'm not opinionated. I'm just always right." Powerful Cholerics operate out of their need for control. They know they are right. Because they offer quick answers, they are often misunderstood. Other people may perceive them as opinionated, while they feel they are simply offering the obvious solution. Why waste time discussing other ideas when they have already come up with the right answer?

Loves a Challenge

Powerful Cholerics love a good challenge. Sandy Sigoloff is a man we're sure is a Powerful Choleric in the perfect position. He turns around ailing companies and brings them back from Chapter 11. Mark Jannot refers to him as the "king of the corporate-salvage business" in his article "Chapter 11, Next Verse" (*American Way,* 1 Mar. 1990). His strength is "his ability to consume information and make decisions on a dime." Only a Powerful Choleric with the ability to be unemotional and function on a strictly intellectual level could "make painful decisions without flinching. At Wickes he chopped 14,000 of 42,000 jobs."

In defense of his actions, Sandy Sigoloff was quoted saying that he "needed to, to save the 28,000 jobs that remained."

Typically, Powerful Cholerics have such focus on the goal that they go to any length to get there. Achieving the goal is the Powerful Choleric ability for which Sigoloff has been hired. He is known as "Sandy the Ax," leading us to think that compassion is not his strong suit. Yet from his own perspective, he *is* compassionate as he eventually saves the corporate prize, but "most observers miss the compassion. If their company's being run by Sigoloff, they're often wiping corporate blood off the floor."

Powerful Cholerics have difficulty resting, love a challenge, and get bored with things that are too easy. In 1980 Sandy Sigoloff "tried handling a healthy business as vice chairman of Kaufman and Broad Inc., a home building and financial services company. The lack of crisis bored him."

Exudes Confidence

Powerful Cholerics exude confidence and can run anything. But their level of confidence is directly tied into their control of the situation. If they are out of control, their confidence fades quickly. They know there is little chance anyone else will be able to handle it.

Janice told us about her dates with Gerald. He single-handedly ran an import/export business out of his house. He worked with companies in Germany and Switzerland with microchips and other telecommunications parts. He liked working out of his house because it allowed him to work round the clock. Since many of the businesses he dealt with were on the other side of the world, he truly did work round the clock. Early in the morning he could be found in his office wearing his bathrobe. The telex was clattering in the background and Gerald could be heard hollering in German to someone on the other end of the phone. Most of Janice's dates with Gerald revolved around business meetings where he had both the cash and the control. He frequently invited her entire family to fancy restaurants in Los Angeles where he gave out Cross pens as if they were party favors.

When Janice turned twenty-one, Gerald was invited to a party with her family. It was held in a restaurant that was about a hundred miles away from his normal entertaining arena. Although he gave Janice a costly gift, he had not bothered to wrap it. He shoved it into her hand with a birthday greeting written on the back of his business card. The suave continental gentleman who had typically been the host with the most was nervous and fidgety all evening. He wasn't on his turf. The restaurant her family had chosen wasn't one he frequented and the maitre d' didn't know him. *They* had chosen what time to meet, where they would go, and what they would eat. Gerald was out of control, and his usual flourish of confidence was gone.

Fearless Activist

Michael Walsh, CEO of Tenneco, seems to be a Powerful Choleric doer. In *Fortune* magazine (18 Nov. 1991), he says, "I use other people to read reports and underline them for me or tell me what they say."

He wastes no time on the details, he just gets down to work. Walsh moved from being the U.S. Attorney in San Diego to Executive Vice President of Cummins Engine to CEO of Union Pacific where he nearly doubled the profits. Typical of the Powerful Choleric businessman, once he got Union Pacific under control, he was ready for a new challenge. He admits "most people would kill" for his Union Pacific job, but at age fifty, the challenge of taking on a whole new set of problems intrigued him. He assumed vast responsibilities as CEO of Tenneco, a conglomerate of six major businesses including chemicals, auto parts, and natural gas pipelines.

Any personality except the Powerful Choleric would be overwhelmed with what Walsh considers an exciting opportunity. He has learned to function in his Powerful Choleric strengths and to overcome his weaknesses, and this self-discipline is what has made him a success.

In reviewing the major difference between Powerful Choleric organization and Perfect Melancholy order, we can narrow it down to a piece of paper. Powerful Cholerics do their organizing quickly and intuitively in their heads. Perfect Melancholies put everything on paper. They need to see it, chart it, and think about it. Perfect Melancholies make fewer mistakes, but Powerful Cholerics are willing to take the chance and move quickly and fearlessly into action.

Overconfident

Confidence in one's ability to function all too often becomes overconfidence, a weakness. Overconfident Powerful Choleric people and organizations risk drowning in their own weaknesses because they *are* usually right. They can scarcely credit it when they are wrong, and they certainly don't like to have the error of their ways pointed out.

Once they've charted a course, they are apt to stick to it even in the face of early indications that it isn't going to work. A Powerful Choleric executive may run roughshod over objections from lower management and continue on a course until a public catastrophe brings the whole house of cards tumbling down. Clearly not all companies that fail are Powerful Choleric organizations run by Powerful Cholerics who've become so confident that they're doing the right thing that they won't listen to anyone else until it's too late. But, from banks to brokerage houses to manufacturing firms of all kinds, we've seen plenty of these overconfident organizations come to ruin in the past several years.

The way to deal with Powerful Cholerics who are overconfident is to deal from their personalities. Strong, sure, and irrefutable evidence (often from outside the company) that the course you're on will come to no good end can work. Present it in a way that they are likely to see the pitfalls, and imagine they found them themselves. Since Powerful Cholerics are usually right and able to be heroes in many situations where their quick thinking saves the day, they have difficulty saying "I'm sorry" or crediting anyone else with saving the day. So don't expect any apologies or credit if you do succeed.

Arrogant

On a navy base where motion pictures were produced for the government, there was an editor known as "Norm the Nazi." Norm was a Powerful Choleric who insisted on complete dedication from those whose work he edited. Even though he wasn't in the military and as a civil service employee could have slid by with casual work, Norm gave it his all and expected the same from everyone else. He would willingly work twelve hours a day and come in on weekends to get a film completed and done right. If he was working on your project after hours, he expected you to be there with him. He had no trouble expressing his opinions and had derogatory names for everyone who didn't see things his way. Norm was proud to be known as "Norm the Nazi." He loved the "power" that came from the fear his nickname instilled in the others.

Fears Losing Control

Powerful Cholerics' only real fear is of losing control. They panic and can go to extremes to keep their grip. Emotionally balanced Powerful Cholerics will desire control but will give and take for the sake of the common good. Those with an obsessive need for control, usually stemming from childhood problems, who would die rather than slip down a rung on the ladder, will stoop to whatever methods necessary to keep a grip on things. They feel the end always justifies the means in getting there.

Hitler was an insecure Powerful Choleric who could never get enough control to make up for his severe psychological problems, which began in childhood. When he got a chance to be a leader, he had the drive to take over the floundering Brown Shirts and give them the hope that they could remake their defeated country and become a powerful force for change. He took control of them far beyond their original expectations. History might have been radically different had he limited his control to taking over a country or two. But he needed more and more to satisfy his extreme lust for power, and he brought the whole world down on himself.

No one reading this is going to be a Hitler, but his emotional needs for loyalty and control can show us what happens when needs become obsessions and we act in frenzy to keep control.

Nervy

A Powerful Choleric woman called Marita to register for the Southern California Women's Retreat and was told that the retreat was sold out. She refused to take no for an answer and insisted she be put on the waiting list. Marita explained that the list was already too long and the woman asked "Couldn't I just show up and walk in?"

"No that wouldn't be fair."

"Well that's what I did last year and it worked."

Cholerics charge in where others fear to tread!

Manipulates Others

Extreme Powerful Cholerics tend to keep control by manipulating people. They may do good deeds for you to gain your allegiance. In their extremes, they may get information on you that almost becomes blackmail. In order to keep their power positions, they seem to need people that are beholden to them or who are afraid that if they stray slightly they will be brought to task or turned in. One Powerful Choleric executive said, "I love to see the fear in their eyes when they're not sure what I know about them. Keeping them scared keeps them loyal."

J. Edgar Hoover, director of the FBI for almost five decades, was almost certainly a Powerful Choleric with an insatiable need for control. He remade the agency in his own image and transformed the unit from a weak and floundering group to the most powerful national police force the United States has ever had. He helped government officials and presidents to gain information they couldn't get themselves, thus endearing himself to them. He intercepted the mails and wiretapped and burglarized when he deemed it necessary without approval or knowledge of the courts or government.

To maintain his powerful position he would quietly let people know that he had information on them that would ruin their careers if it ever got out. This frightened them into supporting him and gave him decades of unchecked authority. He was unforgiving, suspicious, and distrustful, and no one wanted to be on his hate list.

In the workplace, we sometimes find a Hoover in charge, intimidating, frightening, and manipulating others. If you are that person and ask "Isn't everyone like this? Isn't this the only way to win?" the answer is no. You may have carried your directorial abilities to an extreme. No one can really love or sincerely admire the Powerful Choleric who manipulates and who finds sadistic joy in pulling other people's strings. Don't turn your excellent leadership skills into negatives.

Production Oriented

Powerful Cholerics have unique abilities that make them assets to any business. They can see the whole picture, make quick decisions, and come to practical solutions. In situations where a new project lead time is short or disaster is immanent, they rise to the occasion and become heroes. If the Powerful Cholerics in your workplace have a good percentage of Popular Sanguine in them also, they will do well working on the road selling and promoting on their own. Their Popular Sanguine side will blossom with the flexibility and the people contact, and their Powerful Choleric nature will see to it that the work gets done. If their secondary personality is more in the Perfect Melancholy direction, they will typically be adept in business settings where they can take a project from inception all the way to completion. They also do higher-quality work if there are enough others available to whom they can delegate lesser tasks.

Super Powerful Cholerics will be best in settings in which they can control their environment. Because compassion is not their strong suit, they are better placed in positions where they don't deal directly with customers or with personnel problems, as they have a tendency to make others feel insecure or stupid.

When there is work to be done, call on Powerful Cholerics. They can accomplish more in a given amount of time than anyone else—especially if it's such a challenge that no one but them could possibly achieve a victory!

CHAPTER **10**

Peaceful Phlegmatic:
Are We Relaxed Yet?

Strengths	Weaknesses
■ calm	■ stubborn
■ adds balance	■ uninvolved
■ witty	■ procrastinates
■ low-key	■ unenthusiastic
■ considerate	■ hard to get moving
■ reliable	■ too peaceful
■ makes peace	■ careless
■ delegates well	■ lacks follow-through
■ steady	■ dislikes change
■ good listener	■ hates conflict
■ effective motivator	
■ kind	
■ consistent	
■ has few enemies	
■ good administrator	
■ likable	

Peaceful Phlegmatics may be the most important pieces of the puzzle. They are the blue sky of life, the gentle breezes that calm the storm. In many workplaces Peaceful Phlegmatics remain constant, calm, and steady amid the chaos and crisis. In a situation where the Powerful Choleric's rude and thoughtless comments have put the Popular Sanguine into an emotional and totally distracted state, and the Perfect Melancholy is deep in depression over a schedule change, the Peaceful Phlegmatic can be counted on to get the job done despite the turmoil. Not only will Peaceful Phlegmatics keep the work moving, but their peaceful nature will bring balance into the entire workplace and pull the other personalities in from their extremes.

Low-Key

As you look at the pieces in the puzzle of your workplace, the Peaceful Phlegmatics may be the least obvious and, therefore, harder to identify. Since they are more naturally in the background of life, they have fewer outstanding features. This concept is true of Peaceful Phlegmatics both in the *visual* pieces of the puzzle and the *various* pieces. While they do have strengths and weaknesses like all the others, their negatives are less offensive because they are less obvious. And their strengths often go unnoticed.

Where Powerful Cholerics may be bossy and domineering, Peaceful Phlegmatics are calm and agreeable. Where Perfect Melancholies are often introspective and hard to please, Peaceful Phlegmatics are flexible and steady. Where Popular Sanguines are flashy and forgetful, Peaceful Phlegmatics are low-key and reliable.

While the various pieces of the other personalities may jump out at you or drive you crazy, the Peaceful Phlegmatics keep their pieces covered under an exterior of calm. Their apparent indifference may often frustrate others, especially Powerful Cholerics who think if you're not moving you're not motivated. One Powerful Choleric boss stated, "We ought to line up all the Phlegmatics and shoot them, because they are the ones who get the rest of us upset!"

Stubborn

Both Powerful Cholerics and Peaceful Phlegmatics have stubborn natures. Sometimes people confuse them because of their strong wills. Powerful Cholerics' wills show through their words, gestures, and attitude. They let you know their opinions frequently and refuse to back down. In contrast, Peaceful Phlegmatics hide their underlying will of iron. They agree with you to save conflict, but they are saying to themselves, "I have no intention of ever doing that." They are quietly stubborn, nodding on the outside but refusing on the inside.

Steady

When AT&T needed to reorganize after going through the turmoil of the Bell System breakup, they brought on a Peaceful Phlegmatic to add stability. *Fortune* magazine, in a cover story by Andrew Kupfer entitled "Bob Allen Rattles Cages at AT&T" (19 June 1989), tells what happened. While the decision makers probably didn't call Bob Allen a Peaceful Phlegmatic, they undoubtedly chose him for his uniquely Peaceful Phlegmatic qualities. He is described as "a good listener." He is "witty, albeit in a subdued sort of way; stubborn, yet smart enough to know when to change; a less than rousing speaker, yet an effective motivator."

Allen took the helm at AT&T at a particularly shaky time. The previous Chairman and CEO, who had been well-loved and was thought of as a "vibrant and dynamic person," had died suddenly. Adding the steadiness of the Peaceful Phlegmatic, Allen has made changes in almost every aspect of AT&T and has passed the decision-making power down the ranks. He says, "I am becoming more comfortable with decision making being much further down in the organization, because that's where the best decisions get made for the customer." Bob Allen had started with the Bell System right out of college and worked his way up.

Peaceful Phlegmatics may often find themselves in positions of power and authority because they are consistent, reliable, and have few enemies.

Makes Peace

Peacemaking is an important part of the Peaceful Phlegmatic personality. This trait is one of the many pieces of the Puzzle that enhances Peaceful Phlegmatics' leadership abilities. Not known for their energy or creativity, Peaceful Phlegmatics in fact can be quite careless and uninvolved if not properly motivated. They are so pleasant and likable that when they fail to come through with the promised changes or don't produce a job on time, they have a unique ability to smooth over the problem.

Guy is the head of a large group of counseling centers. Like Bob Allen, he is typically good at hiring people to fill in his areas of weakness. "Staff your weaknesses" has been Guy's motto. This Peaceful Phlegmatic is a good administrator who delegates well, but changes in the economic climate have caused a cutback in personnel. Now Guy is almost singlehandedly responsible for running the whole operation and making the decisions. Like many Peaceful Phlegmatics, Guy likes to postpone the decision-making process in the hope that the problem will go away. Sometimes it does, but in this tense time his organization is operating like a ship without a rudder. At meetings with his therapists, he needs his peacemaking ability as they are all unhappy. Issues they had previously discussed have gone unsolved. He just doesn't follow through.

Somehow Guy needs to cut the financial corners differently and bring on a Powerful Choleric/Perfect Melancholy who can be his right hand—attend meetings with him, help with decision making, advise him on the feasibility of planned action, and follow up on the promises he's made. This additional staff person could handle the day-to-day business duties and free Guy up for the relational responsibilities at which he excels. At the moment, he is trying to be all things to all people and violating his own sound principle, "Staff your weaknesses."

Good Administrator

As one of the managing partners of an accounting firm Bill has used the Personality Puzzle as the prime tool in establishing unity. A Peaceful Phlegmatic himself, he wants above all else to have harmony among the staff. He doesn't organize motivational meetings as the Powerful Choleric might. He quietly meets with each partner individually. At these unscheduled and unstructured sessions, he explains the Personality Puzzle to each one and then talks about the emotional needs of all the rest.

His slogan is "Lead into their strengths." He shows them how trying to change other people generally leads to failure. But observing their strengths and talents and leading into these abilities will increase efficiency and harmony. Understandably there are no Popular Sanguines in this office where perfection in calculations is of prime importance. There are many Perfect Melancholies and a few Peaceful Phlegmatics and Powerful Cholerics.

John is a Super Powerful Choleric and a senior partner. Bill has learned that, in order to insert some of his own ideas, he should start by reviewing John's brilliance in earlier concepts meetings. Then he can successfully add things that will make those thoughts even better. As a rule, if you can feed Powerful Cholerics additions to their own ideas, they will usually accept these bits of wisdom and implement them into their plans. You must be willing to not get credit when these ideas come out later as the Choleric's own. Bill says that being Peaceful Phlegmatic helps him create plans for the benefit of the business without needing credit.

Jerry is a younger Powerful Choleric. He wants his own way and is willing to fight to the death rather than back down. The day Bill stepped into the hall to find John and Jerry eye to eye, arguing loudly over which one was right, Peaceful Phlegmatic Bill said, "It looked as if they were about to punch each other out!"

He pulled Jerry into his office and explained that John, as the senior partner, would always win and that to fight him would ultimately bring on Jerry's corporate death. "When you have a disagreement with John," Bill stated, "get over on his side and start adding to his plan. Play into his strengths." As Jerry learned to play to John's strengths, John has changed his opinion of Jerry. Instead of seeing him as a young upstart, he now values his opinion and will occasionally even ask for it. This is a far cry from fighting in the hall.

Bill has a Perfect Melancholy partner, Grant, who tends to work more slowly than the other partners because of his desire to do things exactly right. Bill discussed with John how Grant's personality type had become an important contribution to the organization. John picked up on that idea.

Jerry came to John recently complaining about Grant, who didn't seem to be carrying his share of the work load. Grant's billable hours were lower than anyone else's and Jerry wanted to read him the riot act. John took great pleasure in sharing with Bill his advice to Jerry. John told Jerry that, under no circumstances, should he "read Grant the riot act." "Instead," John said, "I told Jerry how important Grant's role in the firm was and that without unity among the entire partner group the firm would disintegrate and begin to go in different directions."

John actually repeated back to Bill what Bill had taught him. He'd forgotten where these principles had come from and thought they were his own.

As Bill shared these concepts with us he concluded that the knowledge and application of the Personality Puzzle in his business had brought a harmony that would not be possible without it. Remember: lead into their strengths, don't look for credit, and they'll love you for your insight.

Too Peaceful

While Peaceful Phlegmatics are great at making peace, sometimes they are too peaceful. Powerful Choleric Pam told me about her Peaceful Phlegmatic husband who is so calm and peaceful that he has several times driven into their driveway, parked the car, opened the door, and dropped off to sleep with one foot out the door. One day he stopped at a train crossing and, while waiting for the train to pass, fell sound asleep. When he woke up an hour and a half later the train was long gone and the traffic was politely driving around him.

Peaceful Phlegmatics often lack enthusiasm and excitement, especially for other people's projects. When Melissa proofreads the promotional materials Marita writes, she marks the changes and places the pages on Marita's desk. As a part Popular Sanguine Marita takes the materials in hand and asks Melissa, "How were they?" She comments blandly, "There were only a few mistakes." Marita says, "No, no. I mean were the questions good? Did they make you want to read the book?" Because Melissa now understands the Personality Puzzle, she is learning to get excited over her proofreading task and give Marita the encouragement she desires.

Low Motivation

As a part of their peaceful nature Peaceful Phlegmatics lack self-motivation. A noted motivational speaker who is a Powerful Choleric himself enjoyed traveling with his assistant because he was attentive and listened well. However this Peaceful Phlegmatic assistant was not functioning in his strengths when the speaker placed him at the book table on the convention floor. Since book sales are a major part of any speaker's income, the person at the table has a key position and needs to encourage people to buy, emphasizing the personal benefits they will receive from the products.

As we observed the Peaceful Phlegmatic assistant standing alone all day, across from our book booth, we could see clearly that he had been placed where he was functioning in his weaknesses. When people approached the table, he would back away instead of moving toward them. When they asked him what tapes to buy he'd say, "They're all good," instead of making an enthusiastic suggestion. When business was slow in the afternoon, he actually put his head on the table and went to sleep. We were aghast at his siesta and wondered what the motivator would have done if he had walked in and found he was paying his assistant to take a snooze.

How important it is to place people in their strengths and not their weaknesses.

Procrastinates

A Peaceful Phlegmatic man named Klaus told me about the network marketing business he and his Powerful Choleric wife Elke run from their home. They started by selling to a few friends and stocking the products in the basement. As the business grew there was a steady flow of shipping cartons. Klaus carried them from the front door down to the basement. Then he hauled them up the stairs again and out the door to the customer. It occurred to him that it would make more sense if he used the spare bedroom on the main floor for the merchandise. But that involved two problems. First, the cat lived in that bedroom, and he didn't want the cat to be upset with him. Second, to make the transfer he would have to carry all the boxes of products upstairs by himself. The thought of all that work caused him to postpone even mentioning his idea for over two years. But, after one exhausting day of moving boxes up and down stairs Klaus gasped out at dinner, "It would be a lot easier if we kept all this stuff in the spare bedroom—if it weren't for the cat."

The minute Elke heard the idea she called in some of the down-line people in her network who came running over. By midnight that very night, the boxes were all upstairs and the cat was downstairs. "If I'd known how easy it would be," Klaus said, "I'd have mentioned it a long time ago."

Peaceful Phlegmatics' stability and peacemaking are an asset to any workplace. If they are in a position they love they can be highly motivated. The trick is finding what motivates Peaceful Phlegmatics.

They do best in positions where a lot of independent action isn't required and the job at hand has some routine. They need to have clearly spelled out deadlines, otherwise a distraction or complication will result in the project being put aside for another day. With good motivation and supervision, Peaceful Phlegmatics can be wonderful assets to the team. Everyone likes them, they stay out of trouble and can be counted on when the going gets tough!

An Experiment in Group Behavior

At a recent CLASS for advanced speakers we conducted an experiment that we may never try again. The idea seemed so practical when we thought it up. Since these people had been to our basic CLASS and had been taught the Personality Puzzle, we felt they would know how to use their social skills in group activity. We had previously taught them how to put together a speech. Now we thought it would be helpful for them to construct a message in a cooperative group effort. It would be a chance to put the *various* pieces into action, much as they might do in their real life workplace.

We placed them at five round tables in groups of eight. We carefully chose magazine ads that presented clear themes they could build their messages on, and we put three of these on each table. We did not review the Personality Puzzle or challenge the participants to heights of brotherly love. We just let it all happen.

The first hurdle came when they had to choose which ad to use in their cooperative construction. At one table a Powerful Choleric reached out quickly, glanced at the three ads, and announced which one was the "right one." Another Powerful Choleric proclaimed, "I'm not doing the one you chose until I see them all." A Perfect Melancholy said, "You didn't let any of us think about it. You can't choose something that fast. This is really upsetting." The Peaceful Phlegmatic added, "I'd like to at least take a look at them." The Popular Sanguine, seeing the start of trouble, added brightly, "This won't be much fun if we fight over it." The Peaceful Phlegmatic pushed the paper back and said, "Okay you decide. I don't really care."

At another table two Powerful Cholerics reached vigorously for the same ad and ripped it down the middle. The Popular Sanguines laughed until the Powerful Cholerics gave them dirty looks. One of the Powerful Cholerics grabbed a second ad and, without reading it, said "We will do this one. This will work." The other Powerful Choleric folded her arms across her chest and put on an obvious pout. A Perfect Melancholy who had tape in her briefcase worked quietly to put the ripped ad together before we would see it. A Peaceful Phlegmatic reached for the third ad to see what it said. The Powerful Choleric with the second ad in hand stated sternly, "Put that down. This is the one we will use." The Peaceful Phlegmatic put it down. A Popular Sanguine added, "I think they're all good!" The Powerful Choleric ignored this remark and flashed her chosen ad (the second one) around the table quickly for the others to see what they were going to do. "There is no use wasting time talking," she affirmed. "We want to be the first ones finished."

At a third table a Powerful Choleric had chosen an ad, told the group she had a brilliant idea, and instructed them to keep quiet so she could write down her outline before she forgot it. They all sat frozen. A Popular Sanguine looked up with her big eyes and shrugged her shoulders slightly at us as we approached as if to say, "I can't believe I've let her shut me up." As soon as the Powerful Choleric had her outline written down, she stood up and announced to the group, "You will love my outline. To make it easier for all of you, I'm going to the office to run off a copy for each of you." She was so thrilled with herself that she had saved the whole group a lot of work, which they were probably not capable of anyway. She was gone before a Popular Sanguine said, "I didn't even get a chance to look at the ads." A Perfect Melancholy muttered, "I don't want a copy of her ideas."

At the fourth table another Powerful Choleric held up the ad she had chosen. She was being kind enough to let the others contribute thoughts. "Write these down," she said to the Perfect Melancholy next to her. A Peaceful Phlegmatic dared to offer quietly, "I have a good idea." The Powerful Choleric smiled condescendingly as she listened briefly to some muddled thoughts. Then she interrupted and stated, "I'll tell you now what she means by that." She took the ideas, made them into an outline that had little relationship to the Peaceful Phlegmatic's thoughts, and presented them to the group. A Popular Sanguine asked, "Can't we talk about these ads before we put the speech together?" "That would only waste time if we all tried to push for our own ideas," said the Powerful Choleric who had put herself in charge.

At the fifth table, where by chance there were four Popular Sanguines, they were laughing and "having a high-old-time," as one told us. We asked if they had chosen an ad yet, and they all talked at once. They wanted to use the Metropolitan Life ad with a popular cartoon character Lucy in the center. "We can have fun with this one." "I've got great ideas for what we could do with it." "I've always loved Lucy," referring to the cartoon. A Perfect Melancholy sat dejected in the middle of all this, mumbling, "They didn't even listen to my ideas. I hate cartoons, and I liked the ad with the path into the woods." One of the Popular Sanguines just laughed and said "Her ideas just won't work. Besides, cartoons are more fun." A Peaceful Phlegmatic put her hands to her ears and said, "This whole group is too loud. Could I move to a different table?"

We surveyed the room from the middle, somewhat stunned, and not believing what we saw. In less than ten minutes, forty Christian leaders hated each other. The Powerful Cholerics shouted to be heard. One stood with her hands placed in the middle of the table, leaning over and pleading, "Listen to me, listen!" Another grabbed a paper out of a Peaceful Phlegmatic's hands and shouted, "No we won't use your outline. You've got your nouns and verbs all mixed up!" The Peaceful Phlegmatic sank back almost in tears. As she headed for the ladies' room, she told us "I think I've got an upset stomach."

One Powerful Choleric stood up, turned her chair around, and sat down with her back to her group. "I don't like what they're doing. I'm just going to write it my way!" One Perfect Melancholy cried out "Why don't we get it down on paper so we can see what we've done?" And another took a Powerful Choleric outline and said, "I'll check it out to see if you have it in the right tenses."

The Peaceful Phlegmatic who thought her group was too loud took her chair to the foyer and settled in with her concordance. When we questioned her exit from her group, she explained, "It just wasn't worth the fight."

One group seemed to have settled in, and when we checked a Popular Sanguine said, "We decided to each work on one point by ourselves to stop the tension."

A Powerful Choleric who was trying desperately to control a group of chatty Popular Sanguines called to us, "If they don't stop talking and get to work, I'm going to end up with gray hair and go mad!"

Here we thought we had a great idea and it had turned into round-table chaos. What we had instead was a small slice of life with Powerful Cholerics trying for instant control, Popular Sanguines giving examples galore, Perfect Melancholies trying to get it all down on paper, and Peaceful Phlegmatics nursing a group headache. Later, in typical Peaceful Phlegmatic understatement, one of them said, "We all got a bit testy with each other."

As we called the whole experiment to a halt, a Popular Sanguine comedian asked if she could do a review of the groups for their enjoyment. She lined up four chairs at a table up front and pointed out "This is the Popular Sanguine chair, this the Powerful Choleric chair. . . ." She then went back and forth changing personality, tone of voice, and gestures and playing all parts.

"I've got a good idea—it'll be fun!"

"That's stupid. We'll use my ad!"

"Can't we think about it?"

"I feel sick."

Finally, the group began to see themselves. The Popular Sanguines laughed; the Powerful Cholerics realized they had hurt the others; the Perfect Melancholies looked ready to cry; and the Peaceful Phlegmatics looked at the Powerful Cholerics as if wondering whether they'd mend their ways and apologize. A few actually did. But most were indirect in typical Powerful Choleric fashion. One said, "I'm the one who went out and got my outlines copied, but I only did it because it was the right thing to do!"

If we ever try this cooperative creativity again, we'll tell them about this group and review the Personality Puzzle with them first. We learned that you can have the greatest tool in the world, but if you don't use it regularly it does you no good. Here's a scenario in which people could use their knowledge. After refreshing their memories, we'd appoint a chairperson for each table and give them only one ad to work from, eliminating initial hostility. We would ask everyone around the table to give their ideas while the others listened. The chairperson would make up the outline from their input. Using the outline, we would have them each take a point, and then all piece it together like a puzzle. We learned a hard lesson that day. Without knowledge, reminders, admonitions, and specific instructions, we all function in our own personality. Under stress our strengths get carried to extremes and become weaknesses.

The Powerful Choleric grabs control and hurts the others.

The Popular Sanguine gets excited and talks compulsively.

The Perfect Melancholy tries to establish order and gets depressed.

The Peaceful Phlegmatic, to keep peace, pulls away and gives up.

Remember when you are involved in any group activity, review the Personality Puzzle and potential problems. "Forewarned is forearmed." Make the instructions clear and specific, and establish leadership right from the beginning. A circus can be fun, but it won't get the work done!

CHAPTER **11**

The Various Combinations

To help you get a clear understanding of each of the various pieces of the Personality Puzzle, we have so far worked each personality profile in its pure sense. As you begin to piece the personalities in your workplace into the puzzle, you may find that many of them seem to be combinations of more than one personality. This is often the case.

There are four basic combinations in the Personality Puzzle. Those who combine two different personality styles may be close to a fifty/fifty split. Or they may be almost all one personality type with a small percentage of another. Or they may be anything in between. Most people do have a secondary part of the puzzle. Whether it is a small portion of what makes them unique or a big percentage is not vitally important in relating to the personalities in your workplace. Simply knowing they're combinations will help you understand them.

Popular Sanguine/Powerful Choleric

As you can see on the accompanying chart, the Popular Sanguine and the Powerful Choleric are natural personality blends. They are both outgoing extroverts who need people.

Pure Popular Sanguines are charming, entertaining, and fun loving but disorganized, naive, and unable to follow through. They may be compulsive talkers who accomplish little.

Pure Powerful Cholerics are goal-oriented, business-minded achievers who feel the end justifies the means and that their way is the only way. They may be compulsive workaholics who are bossy and controlling.

The combination person will be someone with Powerful Choleric drive and Popular Sanguine charm to take away some of the typical Powerful Choleric harshness. The Popular Sanguine humor tempers the extreme need to be in charge and relaxes the feeling that the world will end if

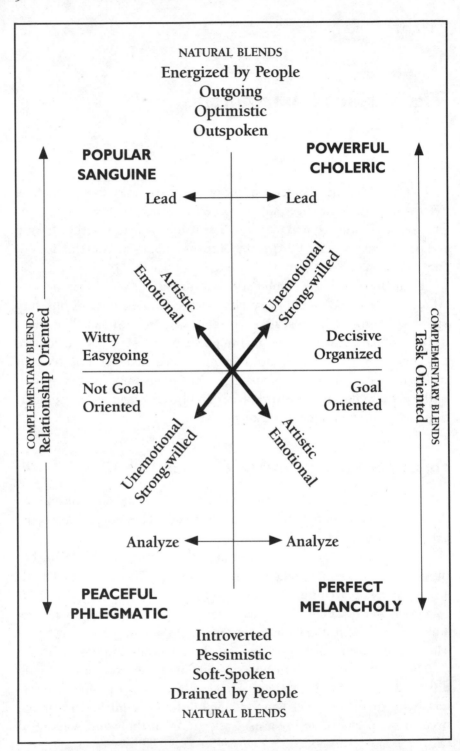

everything doesn't get done today. The Powerful Choleric drive will goad the Popular Sanguine part into finishing what's been started. This combination produces consistent workers who have fun while getting things done. Since both Popular Sanguines and Powerful Cholerics are optimists they have faith that in the long run everything will work out all right. They are both energized by the presence of people and can keep going indefinitely as long as someone is around to praise their good works.

Powerful/Popular Ann Richards

Ann Richards burst onto the national political scene as the keynote speaker at the 1988 Democratic Convention. She let everyone know she was a person in charge of all she surveyed. Her Powerful Choleric nature was obvious to us as she tossed off acid-toned barbs and political insults. But her Popular Sanguine electric twinkle and wild sense of humor shot out like fireworks at a Fourth of July picnic. Here was a tough cookie having fun while stabbing the opposition.

Richards received far more attention and press coverage than Michael Dukakis, a combination Perfect Melancholy and Peaceful Phlegmatic. And the convention went steadily downhill after her magnetic presentation. The only other bright spot came from Jesse Jackson, who seems to be a Popular Sanguine, cheering the crowd on with evangelistic fervor and screaming, "Keep hope alive!"

It was obvious from that convention that Ann Richards was destined for political leadership. She dared to run for governor of Texas against a millionaire who appeared to be a sure-fire winner. He was the model of what Texas used to think a real man should be—a rich, tough rancher and oil baron. What Clayton Williams didn't realize was that times have changed and insulting women is no longer funny. When a surprise thunderstorm hit his house in the midst of a press conference, Williams sealed his fate with an ill-chosen and insulting remark, "Thunderstorms and rape are a lot alike. Once you know it's inevitable, you might as well relax and enjoy it."

When this story hit the headlines, all of William's money couldn't salvage his campaign. Underdog Ann Richards became the first female elected governor of Texas. She quickly took control and made all the unpopular, but necessary, moves. As a practical, powerful personality, Richards is more interested in the process of governing than in the policy.

She is determined to show that government can work and that women aren't weak. She knows herself and her position well enough to know that she can't be so strong that people will rebel against her, nor can she throw out all of the traditions that Texas is steeped in. Treading this middle line is not easy for a Powerful Choleric who would like to throw out all the dummies. As she faced an unhappy and gloomy legislature, Richards looked up brightly and said, "I'm having the time of my life" (*Texas Monthly,* May 1991). Oh, how the Powerful Choleric loves to get a hold on an impossible situation and then solve it!

The Popular Sanguine part of her nature is having fun being in charge. She has a star quality that lights up a room and she wears bright colors that add to her Popular Sanguine personality. Her sense of humor and natural timing take the edge off of her remarks and make acceptable what could be insulting. Like Ronald Reagan she seems Teflon-coated. Negatives slip right off her, leaving her successes standing in the sunlight.

But what happens when people with this combination blunder around in their weaknesses? They might be compulsive talkers, insensitive to other people's needs, rude bossy tyrants desperate to be in control.

Popular/Powerful Boris Yeltsin

Boris Yeltsin, President of the Republic of Russia, seems to be a Popular Sanguine/Powerful Choleric mix. He has certainly publicly functioned in both his weaknesses and his strengths. Coming from a family that shared a wooden hut with nineteen other families, all sleeping on the floor and huddled together with the goats, Boris Yeltsin, in a way, took pride in his extremely humble beginnings. "We had only one aim in life," he says, "to survive!"

"Despite these hardships," Yeltsin continues in his autobiography, *Against the Grain* (Summit Books, 1990), "I always stood out from the other students—especially because of my energy and drive. From first grade on, I was elected class leader, even though I went to several different schools. I did well at my studies and got top marks in my exams. But my behavior was less praiseworthy. In all my years of school I was the ringleader, always devising some mischief."

Because he worked harder than others and saw possibilities where others saw problems, Yeltsin moved up the shaky ladder of Communist success. His pattern was always to set a goal and go beyond it. He wasn't afraid to work and he put a high value on physical fitness. A journalist said, "Pure physical stamina is Yeltsin's most important asset because if he weren't physically fit, he simply could not perform the task he has set for himself. His daily schedule would make a normal man collapse" (*Vanity Fair,* Oct. 1991).

Yeltsin's Popular Sanguine charm made him well-loved and helped him both in and out of trouble throughout his life. When Gorbachev tried to put the threatening Yeltsin into political exile, the move had the opposite effect and made him a hero. The more Gorbachev pushed against him, the more the people loved Yeltsin.

When he came to the United States for the first time, Yeltsin didn't realize the emphasis we place on manners and protocol. He became the proverbial bull in the china shop. He seemed pompous, overbearing, ego centered, ill-mannered, loud, and coarse. He made unfortunate attempts at humor in the presence of Barbara Bush. What was appealing to the Russian peasants was appalling in Washington.

According to *U.S. News and World Report* (2 Sept. 1991), after reading his critical reviews, Yeltsin analyzed his behavior and made a conscious choice to stop functioning in his weaknesses and to improve his image. He hired a speech teacher, watched footage of his presentations, and stopped drinking. When the attempted coup came in August 1991 he seized the opportunity with panache. As the White House of the Russian Republic was surrounded by tanks and the military was claiming victory, Yeltsin took the big chance. Unarmed and in a civilian suit he strode out into the face of the troops, climbed upon an attacking tank, and stood tall in the face of danger. His Powerful Choleric side rose to the sense of danger, and his Popular Sanguine side rose to the drama. As the whole world watched on satellite, Boris Yeltsin became an instant hero, a legend in his own time.

Powerful Choleric/Perfect Melancholy

Another common combination is the Powerful Choleric and the Perfect Melancholy. Since they are both task-oriented types the two personalities combine into a wonderful worker. When you find a Powerful Choleric and Perfect Melancholy blend, you will be able to determine whether they are more Powerful Choleric or Perfect Melancholy by their orientation to people. If they like to be out front and need people, they are a higher percentage Powerful Choleric. If they are more quiet and prefer the background, Perfect Melancholy is probably the dominant piece in their personality puzzle.

When a person is this combination of power and perfection those around had better watch out. These people want things done their way now *and* perfectly. This master manipulator combination is the most controlling of all types.

Pure Powerful Cholerics are determined to be in charge but have little concern for details. They are impulsive, bored by trivia, and sure everything will turn out all right as long as they're in control. Pure Perfect Melancholies are deep, thoughtful, analytical, pessimistic, and convinced that if anything is worth doing it's worth doing right. When these personalities blend, both the intensity of purpose and insistence on perfection increase greatly. The good part is that these people can achieve just about any goal they set better than anyone else could hope to. The bad part is that they will overwhelm everyone and not listen to any opposing opinions.

Powerful Cholerics can adapt to others if the outcome will benefit them in the long run. Because of the difference in outlook, the Powerful Choleric optimistic and the Perfect Melancholy pessimistic, this person has mood swings. The Powerful Choleric part is high on life when things are progressing and under control but can plummet quickly into a Perfect Melancholy depression when there are signs of defeat. These super achiever/perfectionists climb corporate ladders quickly and often become the CEOs. But those addressing them have to check on what humor they're in each day before daring to bring up any difficult problems.

In the best situations the Perfect Melancholy in these people tones down the Powerful Choleric arrogance and the Powerful Choleric part will keeps the Perfect Melancholy moving instead of contemplating. In the area of personal relationships, they tend to use people for their own gain and throw them away when they don't measure up or are no longer needed. These people have a limited sense of humor and no time for fun. If you don't see it their way "you're history."

Powerful/Perfect Katharine Hepburn

Katharine Hepburn is, in our analysis, Powerful Choleric with a touch of Perfect Melancholy depth. She has always done her own thing in Hollywood. She would rather not be in a movie than take on a role she didn't believe in. Her feisty, independent spirit has often caused her to be a loner. She seems to accept the withdrawn pensive life of the Perfect Melancholy.

Her Powerful Choleric desire for control caused her first and only husband to change his name from Ludlow Ogden Smith to Smith Ogden Ludlow because she didn't want to be plain Mrs. Smith. In her book, *Me: Stories of My Life* (Knopf, 1991), Hepburn tells how she controlled just about everyone but Spencer Tracy. He was her one true love, but he was married to someone else. She was willing to modify her opinions when she was with Tracy. "He didn't like this or that. I changed this or that. Food—we ate what he liked. We did what he liked. We lived a life which he liked. This gave me great pleasure."

Powerful/Perfect John Sununu

John Sununu, former White House Chief of Staff, is called the Pit Bull. *Business Week* (28 May 1990) says "his bite is as bad as his bark." It sums up what we see as his Powerful Choleric part, "When he is angry with political foes or, more often, with ill-informed bumblers, his eyes narrow to slits, and his reputed temper erupts in an acid-bath of scorn." Could there be any stronger words?

Sununu seems to be happiest when embroiled in controversy. He seems to enjoy agitating friend and foe alike. In the above article, he was called cruel, indelicate, lacking finesse, a street fighter, an arm-twister, a tough guy.

His Perfect Melancholy side shows in his brilliant retentive mind, his ability to assimilate facts, and his prodigious memory for details. He reads and digests every book and briefing paper that appears before him. He throws out accurate, academic, information at the right moment, intimidating even those who wrote the material. As a former engineering professor, Sununu is a natural for remembering charts and figures. He seems to pride himself on always being right. According to *Business Week,* one colleague said, "He's an extremely adaptive and intelligent guy who asks the right questions and strikes terror into the hearts of Congress and the Cabinet."

Sununu doesn't seem to have any heart for the clubby games Washington insiders play. His brusque style and arrogance have managed to antagonize just about everyone except George Bush, who defended him to the end. President Bush, seemingly a Peaceful Phlegmatic, needs a few tough-skinned people around to take the flack and absorb political blows so that he can smile and stay above the fray in his own kinder and gentler world.

In November 1991, Sununu took it upon himself to improve upon the President's speech. He penciled in some changes that were typed into the final copy, and the President read them without realizing they were opposite thoughts from what he meant to say. Sununu was living on borrowed time, and the question was how long his reign would last.

Perfect/Powerful Clarence Thomas

Clarence Thomas is a Perfect Melancholy with some Powerful Choleric. There's some of the brooding contemplative, compassionate humility apparent to reporters as they have watched him, but there is also that Powerful Choleric quick anger, fire-in-the-eyes glance. There is evidence of his impulsive, hot-headed and opportunistic approach to life that makes people question "Will the real Clarence Thomas please stand up?"

When asked about his religious background—born Baptist, raised by Catholic nuns, and now an Episcopalian—Thomas replied, "God is all right. It's the people I don't like" (*Newsweek,* 16 Sept. 1991).

We see a Perfect Melacholy combined with the Powerful Choleric. He himself realizes that he is a divided personality. "I am the product of hatred and love." He grew up in the racial bigotry of his southern town with loving grandparents who said, "You can make it, but first you must endure." He did more than endure; he lifted himself up and, in his Powerful Choleric mode, said to himself "I'll show them." And he did! He progressed from poverty in Pin Point, Georgia, to the peak of power on the bench of the Supreme Court.

"Conflict and confusion have been Thomas's signature," according to *Newsweek.* "Clarence Thomas's life is a puzzle that offers the pieces for prediction: What type of justice might he make and what kind will he dispense?"

Before any scandal hit the nomination of Clarence Thomas, his low-key and thoughtful personality was beginning to show. As Thomas stood on the lawn of the Bush summer home and with tears in his soulful eyes thanked the nuns who had taught him as a child, his emotional sensitivity and gentle spirit were displayed. When *Newsweek* calls his life "contradictory" they actually descibe the contrast of the Perfect Melancholy and the Powerful Choleric in one person.

"He is the juridical embodiment of Newton's third law: For every Clarence Thomas revealed in this anecdote or that speech, there seems to be an equal and opposite Clarence Thomas somewhere else."

Everyone is a puzzle but knowing the natures of the different personality pieces gives us an understanding of what looks like conflict and confusion to others.

Perfect Melancholy/Peaceful Phlegmatic

Since both the Perfect Melancholy and the Peaceful Phlegmatic tend to be introverted and pessimistic they are a natural combination personality. The Perfect Melancholy and Peaceful Phlegmatic combination produces perfectionists who want to avoid problems. This dual desire causes these people to be fighting within themselves: "To make this project perfect will cause conflict. I don't want any kind of confrontation, but I can't do less than my best. Oh woe is me! What shall I do?"

This constant inner conflict accentuates the Peaceful Phlegmatic indecision and keeps the Perfect Melancholy part depressed. This "Should I or shouldn't I?" debate may paralyze these people and keep them from ever getting on with the projects at hand. The Peaceful Phlegmatic tendency to procrastination combined with the Perfect Melancholy need to think everything over thoroughly can prevent progress of any type.

Perfect/Peaceful Hamlet

Shakespeare's Hamlet provides a created example of the "Melancholy Dane" and the Peaceful Phlegmatic prince. When Hamlet first appears he is in deep grief over the death of his father the king and the instant and incestuous marriage of his widowed mother to his uncle. Hamlet is an idealist and abnormally sensitive to the feelings of others. Depressed, brooding, and indecisive, Hamlet doesn't know what action to take, if any, about his father's suspected murder.

In his moments of Perfect Melancholy introspection and Peaceful Phlegmatic fear of confrontation, Hamlet gives his well-known soliloquy and asks himself, "To be, or not to be: that is the question. Whether 'tis nobler in the mind to suffer the slings and arrows of outrageous fortune, or to take arms against a sea of troubles, and by opposing end them" (Act 3, Scene 1).

Should he keep his fears and anguish to himself and pretend his father died of natural causes or should he take action against his uncle or should he kill himself and end it all? Which is the noble way? And what is it like after we die? "To die; to sleep; no more; and by a sleep to say we end the heart-ache and the thousand natural shocks that flesh is heir to. 'Tis a consummation devoutly to be wish'd" (Act 3, Scene 1).

For Hamlet, being dead seems to be an escape from the thousand natural shocks we all face in life. But does he dare take the chance?

"But that the dread of something after death, the undiscover'd country from whose bourn no traveller returns, puzzles the will and makes us rather bear those ills we have than fly to others that we know not of? Thus conscience does make cowards of us all" (Act 3, Scene 1).

Who knows what heaven or hell is really like, he ponders, for no traveler has returned. So perhaps it's better to bear our current problems than to fly off against our sea of troubles and end it all. Hamlet's soliloquy reveals the depths of his misery and the mental debate he is having within himself. He settles for more Perfect Melancholy introspection and more Peaceful Phlegmatic procrastination. Does the slow self-examination sound like anyone you know?

Perfect/Peaceful Audrey Hepburn

The award-winning actress Audrey Hepburn is, in our analysis, an elegant example of the combined Perfect Melancholy and Peaceful Phlegmatic. She has the quiet strength and complex depth of the Perfect Melancholy, beautifully blended with the regal serenity and shy smile of the Peaceful Phlegmatic. Her brilliant mind and proficiency in several languages give her confidence in her abilities, but her Peaceful Phlegmatic humility keeps her from drawing attention to herself.

A Popular Sanguine or Powerful Choleric of her stature would dress in the latest flashy designer ensemble, arrive late, and create a grand entrance. But Audrey doesn't need the adulation of the crowds. She's easily content staying quietly at home in Switzerland and doing her own marketing at the small town stores. She doesn't need the latest gowns for her self-worth and yet she is always considered a fashion statement. On a six-city tour of the United States she took only two suitcases, dressed daily in simple black with pearls and diamond earrings and was considered the best-dressed woman in every setting. She has become a legend of elegance without ever trying to be a star.

Hepburn was eleven when the Germans invaded Holland. During the war she and her mother suffered from anxiety, lack of food, and numerous diseases. Because of what she calls her five years of malnutrition and her subsequent aid from the United Nations Relief and Rehabilitation Administration, Audrey Hepburn is deeply committed to her charity work with UNICEF, giving back what was given to her.

Contrary to what we might think, she is ill at ease in doing public speaking for UNICEF. "The whole thing terrified me and still does. I wasn't cut out for this job. It doesn't mean that because I was an actress I got over being an introvert. Acting is something quite different from getting up in front of people over and over again in so many countries. Speaking is something that is terribly important" (*Vanity Fair,* May 1991).

Audrey Hepburn takes her service seriously and has studied up on all of the 128 countries she has visited. She wants to know what she's talking about. She doesn't just lend her name to UNICEF as some stars might do for media credit, she goes to places like Bangladesh and sees the starving children in the streets.

The positive part of this combination is that the Peaceful Phlegmatic laissez-faire attitude mellows the Perfect Melancholy need to persist until reaching perfection, and the Perfect Melancholy urge for organization and achievement motivates the Peaceful Phlegmatic to action.

Peaceful Phlegmatic/Popular Sanguine

The Peaceful Phlegmatic and Popular Sanguine combination is perhaps the most engaging and delightful. Both personalities are relationship-oriented, and neither one has any great drive for achievement. They both put having a good time over any serious projects in life. They both have a sense of humor, and when combined they become the show-offs with a quick wit and the ability to toss off a line that will bring down the house. Peaceful Phlegmatic humility tones down the Popular Sanguine self-centered nature, and Popular Sanguine's colorful conversation brings Peaceful Phlegmatic out of the shell.

As you observe those in your workplace and see combined Popular Sanguines and Peaceful Phlegmatics, you can determine their more prominent personality by their desire to be with people. If they become suddenly energetic at the mention of a party, they are probably more Popular Sanguine than Peaceful Phlegmatic. If they like to party, but only if the party comes to them, their Peaceful Phlegmatic side is the prevailing personality.

Whichever way the percentages fall, Peaceful Phlegmatic combined with Popular Sanguine makes an appealing personality. Powerful Choleric women almost always go for the man who has this laid-back humor combined with cool, detached charm.

Not all Peaceful Phlegmatic and Popular Sanguine men can hold life together. Women are attracted to them until they marry one and find he is irresponsible, unmotivated, and unconcerned over money matters. Nothing is bad enough to get upset over. Let's just look the other way and hope it goes away.

Whether this combination is male or female, neither one should be put in control of the finances. No matter what course on financial management this person has attended, don't hand over the checkbook. The Peaceful Phlegmatic and Popular Sanguine's desire for fun and attention will win over fiscal prudence every time.

Popular/Peaceful Warren Beatty

Warren Beatty seems to us to be an example of the Popular Sanguine and Peaceful Phlegmatic who has used his combined strengths to great box-office success. He possesses an abundance of Popular Sanguine charm and can lure women to his side with a twinkle of the eye. Yet he is reserved, cool, sometimes aloof. It is said that he is discreet about his indiscretions. An article in *Vanity Fair* (Nov. 1991) describes his Popular Sanguine and Peaceful Phlegmatic nature quite well. "He is so friendly but elusive, as vain as molybdenum steel in the tensile strength of his ego, yet as modest and haunted as an unsuccessful actor at the prospect of failure. . . . Nothing is harder to locate than the soul in people who possess charm."

Warren Beatty has been able to accentuate his strengths and minimize his weaknesses—the key to making the best of one's personality.

It is often difficult to probe into the soul and emotions of Peaceful Phlegmatics because they take pride in hiding how they really feel about anything, and with the addition of Popular Sanguine, they are able to cover any pain with charm and deny any unpleasant reality.

On a talk show the day that his film *Bugsy* was released, Warren Beatty exhibited his Popular Sanguine appeal as he twinkled into the camera while lounging in Peaceful Phlegmatic style on a large, comfy chaise. Regis, observing the presence and posture of Beatty, asked Kathie Lee, "What is it about him that turns you on?"

She summed up his combination Popular Sanguine and Peaceful Phlegmatic demeanor perfectly even though it's doubtful she understood the Personality Puzzle. "He has lots of charm, and he's a great listener. Women love a man who listens."

This should give courage to you Peaceful Phlegmatic men who don't feel you have much to say. Practice listening. Women love it.

Peaceful/Popular Willie Nelson

Willie Nelson was raised by his paternal grandparents after his parents abandoned him. Early in life, he and his sister won talent shows singing gospel numbers in local Texas churches. He began writing music at a young age.

As he traveled and sang in bars and night clubs, he picked up losers who loved him and put together a motley band. These people needed something to believe in, and Willie had the Peaceful Phlegmatic and Popular Sanguine cool charm that attracted allegiance. They needed a king and he needed a court. They lived on the road, sang for food, and slept in their cars. Willie's gang became his family, and he seemed to be closer to them than he had ever been to any of his four wives and assorted children. Like his parents who had left him, he didn't see a need to stay at home and be a real father.

By 1978, when CBS released "Stardust" and it became a triple platinum platter, he was earning $2.1 million a year. Up to that point he had spent the money each day that he had earned each night. He never worried about tomorrow, but now he had more money to play with than he ever imagined possible. He bought houses and cars for himself and his friends and didn't give a thought to the future or to his finances. His daughter,

Lana, tried to stop his reckless spending. But he believed that a man should live for the moment, take what comes, enjoy it to the hilt, and never look back. Willie's bus became a perpetual party place. And when asked if he shouldn't do some kind of financial planning he replied "Never. It's more fun if we don't" (*Texas Monthly*, May 1991).

Fun ended for Willie when the IRS, who kept better books than he did, slapped down a $16.7 million bill for back taxes. The Popular Sanguine part of Willie thought he'd write a few songs and sing them to the IRS who would love and forgive him. His Peaceful Phlegmatic nature refused to worry about the consequences. According to the *Vanity Fair* article about Willie (Nov. 1991) and the many magazines and newspapers which covered his plight, the IRS wasn't interested in his talent, and they swooped down and confiscated his seventy-six acre personal country club, his recording studio, all his tapes, and even his bronzed baby shoes. Willie still has his guitar and a few friends and he's back where he started from "On The Road Again."

Various and Combined

Reading about these very different individuals gives us insight into using the tools of the Personality Puzzle. Using these tools doesn't limit our perception or put people into boxes. The people we describe here in each of the combined categories have few similarities, particularly in the details of their lives. Yet looking at them from the perspective of the Puzzle gives us clues about how given personalities will act and react in different work situations.

We can see objectively how people succeed when they are functioning in their strengths and why they fail when they operate in their weaknesses. We can also see how to succeed ourselves by appealing to the strengths of those we work with. We can begin to deal with others from our own strengths without letting our strengths turn into weaknesses or annoying others by treating things too lightly (Popular Sanguine), threatening them by coming on too strong (Powerful Choleric), boring them with details (Perfect Melancholy), or frustrating them by avoiding issues (Peaceful Phlegmatic). We can begin to fit the pieces of our own particular Personality Puzzle together for a more harmonious environment and better business success.

PART THREE

The Valuable Pieces

*How to Use
the Personality
Puzzle in Your
Workplace*

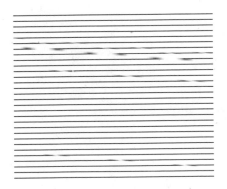

CHAPTER 12

Fitting the Valuable Pieces Together

By now we hope that you have been able to piece together the personalities in your workplace. You've spotted the chatty one with the messy desk as a Popular Sanguine, and you now understand why everyone loves her so much that they put up with her loud and forgetful nature. You have identified the meticulously dressed computer specialist who comes in to solve problems as a Perfect Melancholy, and you now realize that no matter how many times he comes in he will never act like family or ask you about yours. You know that the salesman who bounds in, checks the stock, writes the order, asks for a signature, and is gone before you had a chance to say hello, isn't overtly rude or antisocial. Rather he is a Powerful Choleric who has a tight schedule with a lot of calls to make. You've learned not to take it personally, as you now understand that the Powerful Choleric doesn't waste time shooting the breeze. You've placed the mellow woman who keeps more to herself and quietly goes about her business, never offending anyone, into the Peaceful Phlegmatic part of the Puzzle.

Through the combination of the *visible* pieces of the Puzzle and the *various* ones, you have pieced together the picture that makes up your workplace. You have a better understanding of what to expect from each of the separate pieces in your workplace puzzle. If you are the boss, this insight will help you make placement decisions. If you are a part of the team, it will give you insight into your coworkers' motivation and behavior.

Will this knowledge help when you have problem people whom you must face every day? What if they don't understand you?

While we cannot force others to change—although we may try—and we can't make them adore us, we can learn to get along with them. Just as each different piece in the Personality Puzzle has *visible* pieces and *various* pieces, they also have *valuable* pieces, which are the keys to understanding and peaceful relationships. Just as each personality has a basic desire—the Popular Sanguine for fun, the Perfect Melancholy for perfection, the Powerful Choleric for control, and the Peaceful Phlegmatic for peace—each also has emotional needs. When you understand the emotional needs of the Personality Puzzle you can give others what they need instead of what you need. This is often difficult to grasp, as many of us grew up learning to "do unto others as you would have them do unto you." When we can change our perspective and do unto others as they would like and not as we wish to do according to our own personality, we can transform relationships.

Filling Other People's Needs

As women have climbed into management positions there has been a softening in social and business interactions. No longer is the dictatorial boss accepted as the norm because command-and-control authority is not producing results. The time has come for Powerful Cholerics to rethink their strategy.

James Autry, president of Meredith Corporation, has already made the change. "I flew jet fighters in the Air Force for four years back in the 1950s. I was as macho as anyone who ever drew a breath," he admits. "I came into business thinking the command-and-control model was the way to get the job done. But what I've come to realize, after twenty-nine years of management, is that what works most often is what is most responsive to people's needs and gives them the freedom to make choices" (*Executive Female*, Sept./Oct. 1991).

Meeting people's needs is always more effective than the didactic "Do it because I said so!"

The average church is loaded with puzzle pieces all trying to find their places with no one who knows how to fit them together. What a tool the personality types could be in the church to help pastors and lay leaders utilize the appropriate people for particular ministry positions. One lady told us how she had observed a situation in her local fellowship involving church ushers.

From the group of ushers one man was selected to stand at the front to greet and welcome those attending the service, answer any questions, and give each person a bulletin. This man was an obvious Perfect Melancholy. He was quiet to begin with, but as each week went by he looked progressively depressed. People had to pluck the extended bulletin from his hand. He didn't talk to anybody. And many wondered what perception of the church this might give visitors.

One time when we visited this church the man was so tired that he was sitting in a chair by the front door, hanging his head and holding the bulletin up! This Perfect Melancholy usher was basically "burned-out" by months of trying to fill a niche that did not come naturally to him. He was ultimately replaced as the greeter by an obvious Popular Sanguine usher who had been feeling stifled in his "sideline" position. In this new assignment, the Popular Sanguine absolutely blossomed and heartily greets everyone who enters the building. What a difference!

The woman who told us this story said, "I used to have the ludicrous misconception that to really serve the Lord within the church, it was more godly to be miserable! At the same time, I wondered why such a small percentage of members actually participated in any ministry, and those who did were often victims of burn-out. If church members could be guided into areas that utilized their particular personality strengths, they would be more willing to volunteer and serve the Lord with gladness rather than taking up their cross daily."

How helpful it would be if churches would make an effort to put people where they belong.

Jenny is a true Popular Sanguine. She works for a manufacturing company and usually handles telephone sales. She loves meeting different people by phone and has become friends with many of them. If their vacation plans bring them to her town, they often stop by just to meet her. Once a year she goes to the annual trade show where she works in the booth, meets new people, and shows them the products. While the trip should be exciting for her, she realized that after a couple of years she was really dreading going to New York.

The first day she did wonderfully, saw some old friends and met new ones. By the third day she really didn't care to meet another person, yet she is a Popular Sanguine who loves people.

Jenny has attended several of our seminars, listened to our tapes, and read the books. She understands the Personality Puzzle well and knows that she is a Popular Sanguine. Since she normally loves the trade shows, she tried to figure out what was wrong.

Jenny's supervisor, Bob, was a Peaceful Phlegmatic. He liked taking her to the trade shows because she did all the people work, and he could relax. But he didn't understand Jenny's personality. He knew she was outgoing and that everyone loved her, but he didn't know she had different needs from his own. He let her do her business and he went about his, going out to lunch with existing clients and making important industry contacts.

Because Jenny had studied the Personality Puzzle, she knew her emotional needs were for attention and approval. Back at the home office she got plenty of strokes from her fellow Popular Sanguine salespeople who applauded each new sale. But there in New York it was just she and Bob. She was so self-motivated that he didn't see any need to get involved. After three days, Jenny was starved for the attention and approval she needed. True the customers liked her, but it wasn't the same as the approval she needed from her boss. She wanted him to notice the sales she had made and praise her for all her hard work.

In the third day of the show, when she was feeling particularly down, she pieced together the problem. When Bob came back, she showed him all the orders she had written while he was gone. He told her it was "nice." Jenny was able to explain to Bob that she would do better if he could get more enthused over her work and that "nice" wasn't motivating. Bob told her that she got enough of that at the office. She was able to show him that she was used to lots of praise, and his lack of it made her want to quit. Throughout the rest of the show Bob was able to muster up enough praise, although from time to time he did need some prodding.

If Bob had understood the concepts of meeting emotional needs from the beginning, he would have been a better manager, the sales might have been even higher, and Jenny would look forward to the next trade show instead of dreading another "down time."

Personality of the Boss

Whatever type of boss you have, understanding his or her personality will help you get along and meet his or her emotional needs. In an article "The Boss from Hell" in *Working Woman* (Dec. 1991) author Julie Lopez states that 75 percent of the managerial staffs surveyed had trouble with their superiors. They didn't understand them, and they felt they all had personality problems. Plus, each manager had the pessimistic feeling that the next boss would probably be worse.

Lopez narrowed down the possibilities. "There are essentially two choices: Either you can bail out or you can work to manage the boss's idiosyncrasies. The goal is to become a constructive ally, to help recognize and deal with the various personality quirks."

The author then divided up the types of bosses and gave descriptions that exemplified the four personalities.

Her Incompetent is similar to the Popular Sanguine, chatting on the phone all day and not having a clue about how to accomplish anything. Answer: Do his work and make him look good. He'll love you.

Her Workaholic is an obvious Powerful Choleric, treating the employees as slaves, expecting everyone to work around the clock. Answer: Do it her way now, but don't be bullied into unreasonable demands.

Her Phantom, similar to the Perfect Melancholy, stays away from the action, leaves an empty chair, and communicates by detailed memos from outer space. Answer: Write back and enumerate all you have accomplished.

Her Wimp describes the Peaceful Phlegmatic. "These are the bosses who can't take charge, try to avoid conflict, and become paralyzed when faced with a decision." Answer: Boost the weakling's confidence, and feed him facts he can use.

In this brief and humorous article Lopez accurately portrays the different personalities and gives helpful hints. We are taking that a lot deeper in showing you why these people are this way. It's so much easier to deal with difficult people when you realize they were born that way, and they are not specifically out to get you. When we understand the emotional needs of those in our workplace, we can fit the valuable pieces into the picture and complete the Puzzle.

CHAPTER 13

The Valuable Popular Sanguine: Look At Me!

As we know, Popular Sanguines are the flashy personality, both in their visible and various pieces of the Puzzle. They are the ones who hide nothing. What you see is what you get. So it is with the valuable pieces of their puzzle. They regularly ask, even cry out, to have their emotional needs met, although most of us are not alert enough to notice.

The most important thing you can do for the Popular Sanguines in your life is give them *attention* and *approval*. Their bright colors and loud voice are really a bid for attention, and their ability to turn on twinkling charm is really a request for approval. While Popular Sanguines may not be consciously aware of this need in their own lives it is still the underlying factor in most of their decision-making processes.

Monica, a Popular Sanguine, was a regional sales manager for a greeting card company. It was a new job for her. She had talked her way into the position even though she had no prior experience in the field. She had a three-month probation period after which, if her sales were good enough, she was to be given a company car.

The parent company was several states away, and Monica functioned without supervision and made her own schedule. When she took over her territory it had three accounts. Two had gone out of business and one owed the company money. After several weeks of charm and hard work, she had over seventy accounts. Each week she packaged up her orders and dropped them in the mailbox. Every other week the company mailed her a check. Since Monica was working toward the car, she wondered if her sales were good enough for their standards. Halfway into her three months she still hadn't heard a word from the company, so she called in hopes of receiving some accolades. She didn't know if anyone had even noticed she was out there.

Instead of giving Monica the praise she'd hoped for, the National Sales Manager simply suggested that she should be making more calls in person and fewer by telephone. She was devastated and wanted to quit right there. But she had no other job lined up and needed the money. So she forced herself to get out there and make those calls. When the end of the three months came, Monica was so burned out from the lack of kudos, she called the company to quit. The National Sales Manager said her car was on its way to her. That very moment, someone was driving it to her home. She told them to keep it.

This relationship didn't have to end this way. Monica started with the great energy and enthusiasm of a Popular Sanguine. Within three short months she had run dry. How could this have been prevented?

If the National Sales Manager had understood Monica's personality and recognized her midway call as a request for attention and approval, he would have praised her for all she had done and told her how much the company appreciated her being able to transform that otherwise dead area. If he had called her each time he got her reports and told her how happy he was with her, Monica's energy would have been restored and she would, perhaps, today be the company's top producer or even the National Sales Manager herself.

Popular Sanguines seem to have an unlimited reserve of energy. But it has to come from somewhere. It generally comes from the attention and approval they get from others. This approval is food to Popular Sanguines, and when they eat it they are restored and refreshed.

Wendy, a Popular Sanguine, came to work for an advertising agency totally depleted. She had been working in an accounting firm where she worked with a group of Perfect Melancholies who didn't appreciate her bubbly nature. In addition, Wendy was in a marriage where she was belittled for anything she did that wasn't perfect. In both major parts of her life, Wendy was surrounded by people who expected perfection. Like all Popular Sanguines, Wendy tried hard to please them and make them like her, but she could never do well enough to get the praise she longed for.

The advertising agency she went to work for was filled with creative Popular Sanguine and Powerful Choleric people. Wendy's job encompassed many small tasks and revolved around answering the incessantly ringing phone. At first Wendy was like a scared mouse, terrified she might do everything wrong. Her coworkers encouraged her, and her Popular Sanguine personality blossomed when she was on the telephone. Clients frequently comment on Wendy's cheerful conversation and say her calls brighten their day. She often takes projects home on weekends to complete on her own time. When she returns with them on Mondays, she is praised and appreciated.

Wendy still has a difficult home life, but now because she has understanding coworkers who feed her needs, her energy has been restored. She looks forward to coming to work and hates to leave. Wendy has had a transformation in her personality and her appearance has even changed. Her coworkers have taken an interest in her. For her birthday they gave her a gift certificate for a permanent and haircut. Once a week she joins some of the others at the local beauty college for a manicure and proudly wiggles her fingers in front of their faces to show off her lovely nails.

Wendy's emotional needs are being met in her workplace. She has grown from a scared mouse to an energetic force that gets her job done and keeps everyone happy at the same time. When we understand the emotional needs of those we work with, we can put the pieces of the Puzzle together so they fit harmoniously.

CHAPTER 14

The Valuable Perfect Melancholy: Understand Me

As Perfect Melancholies' goal is perfection, their emotional need is for *order* and *sensitivity*. Like Popular Sanguines, Perfect Melancholies are emotional people. The difference comes in what evokes the emotion in them. Perfect Melancholies' emotion is often shown through sensitivity. Popular Sanguines will be sensitive if someone says something that hurts them, but the Perfect Melancholy will be moved to tears by footage of starving children in Africa.

While they desire "perfection" in their professional lives they also need their personal lives to be in order, and they will appreciate others who are sensitive to their needs.

One day two dozen red roses appeared on Keri's desk. While Keri is a Perfect Melancholy, she works with several Popular Sanguines who wanted to know all the details. The appearance of two dozen red roses was more than they could stand. Since, as a Perfect Melancholy, Keri didn't share the source of the roses, the Popular Sanguines were left to assume romantic involvement. They giggled and secretly began wedding plans on the slim evidence of the roses. Whenever the salesman who brought the roses called, the Popular Sanguines made a big fuss.

As the Perfect Melancholy who doesn't like to expose her private life, Keri didn't appreciate the assumptions. Finally she was so uncomfortable she asked the others to stop their matchmaking comments.

In fact, their donor had previously made a sales call to a wholesale florist and, since Keri was in charge of purchasing a large system from him, he appreciated her business. The roses were simply a gesture of his appreciation, a smart business move. The frequency of his visits was to analyze the firm's needs and then implement the system. While there may have been a tinge of romantic interest, the relationship was a professional one and certainly didn't call for wedding plans. But the curious Popular Sanguines couldn't resist a possible story, and they were insensitive to Keri's needs.

You will improve your relationships with Perfect Melancholies in your workplace when you understand their natures and are sensitive to their needs. Joseph is a finish carpenter who is highly skilled at the meticulous details of fine cabinetry. As a part of one of his big jobs, he was to supervise all of the finish work on a condo conversion project. The condos needed to be completed in time for the seasonal tourist traffic. Joseph was working hard to get them done in time, but creating perfection takes time. His boss quenched his desire to do the job when he told him that it didn't need to be that good. These were only vacation home condos, and no one would notice if they were perfect or not. Joseph's Perfect Melancholy nature struggled with doing a job that wasn't his best. Finally he had to leave the project. Today, he is in a better position for his personality. He is working in a shop that does only fine carpentry work. His boss is extremely happy with his work and would never think of asking Joseph to compromise his high quality.

Maureen was a counselor in a Christian high school. It was a new school, and she was involved in setting many of the standards for the whole school. She knew these standards would be with the school for years to come, and she worked very hard to be sure that they were fair to everyone. One of the projects on which she labored the most was the grading system. There was a debate over whether to use "pluses" and "minuses" in conjunction with the letter grades. Maureen made the choice, and the system functioned smoothly until one time when she was out sick.

A parent called in and complained that she wasn't happy with the system and made quite a fuss. The school principal was a Peaceful Phlegmatic who was uncomfortable being attacked and who gave in to the pressure. While Maureen was out for just two days, her weeks of work were thrown out the window because of one complaint. When Maureen returned after her brief absence to find that all her efforts to be fair had been ignored and simply replaced, she was devastated and ready to quit on the spot.

She liked her work, but the principal's lack of sensitivity was demoralizing. Fortunately, Maureen didn't quit. She talked things over with her boss, and after the discussion, her system was put back in place as the standard. How could this problem have been avoided in the first place? If the principal had understood Maureen's Perfect Melancholy personality and used that knowledge in this situation, he would have been sensitive to Maureen's work on the system. Since she is a Perfect Melancholy, she did put a lot of thought and effort into the decision and she must have had good reason for finally settling it as she did. Therefore, when the parent called, the principal might have said something like, "I see your concerns, but Maureen put a great deal of thought into the final system we have adopted. She is out sick right now. When she returns I will check out your concerns, and either she or I will get back to you." Instead of pulling the rug out from under Maureen, this would have both accorded the proper respect to her preparation and handled the problem.

When you are working with Perfect Melancholies, realize that they always do their best and that they have specific reasons motivating their actions. Unlike Popular Sanguines who may make a choice on a whim, Perfect Melancholies will have thought through every option and made their choice to be fair to everyone.

Marita and her friend Marilyn work together every year to put on the Southern California Women's Retreat, which over a thousand women attend. As the Popular Sanguine part of the team, Marita is responsible for coming up with the program ideas and creating the brochure. Marilyn handles all of the money and the registration duties. Those who know them are amazed that two people of such obvious opposite personalities can work together. An understanding of each other's personalities and especially of the valuable pieces of the Puzzle have allowed them to work together peaceably for years.

Their work relationship was put to the test a few years ago when Marilyn had made the biggest bank deposit of the year. The early registration deadline had just passed, and there were several hundred registrations to process. Marilyn made the deposit in the night drop as she often did. The next day she called to verify that the deposit had gotten in all right. The bank had no record of it.

If Marilyn was any of the other personalities she would have handled it differently, but as a Perfect Melancholy she knew it was her fault. "Should haves" played over and over in her head. "I should have hand carried it into the bank. I'm no good at this. I don't know why Marita has me do this. I'm a failure."

When Marilyn called Marita and, through tears, told her what had happened, Marita knew to be sensitive to the Perfect Melancholy needs. They discussed the problem and found that Marilyn had several double check systems. She had a list of every person whose check was in the lost deposit; she knew the check number and the amount it was written for. Marita assured her that the money wasn't needed for months, and they could contact those whose checks were in the deposit and get replacements.

A few minutes after hanging up the phone, Marita called Marilyn back. She said, "I just have one more thing to say: It's not your fault and don't you dare quit!" She knew that as a Perfect Melancholy, Marilyn would be thinking it was all her fault and would want to quit. Marita's understanding of the Perfect Melancholy personality saved the relationship, and they have continued to work well together. We can all learn to lead into other people's personalities and not out of our own.

In addition to sensitivity, Perfect Melancholies also need order. They can't function amid chaos and will appreciate the space and distance that will allow them order. Leslie, a Perfect Melancholy, went to work in a Popular Sanguine office. She came to fill a newly created position and was appalled when she found the desk she took over was still filled with papers that had been in the drawers for years. Leslie had no calendar or "in" and "out" baskets. The pens that were in her desk all bore the logo of popular hotel chains, and they frequently disappeared from her desk while she was in the bathroom or on breaks.

Her boss tried to accommodate Leslie's needs and got her all the desk accessories necessary for her to function properly. Yet, even with the right accessories, Leslie found the Popular Sanguine office too disorderly to work in. Four Popular Sanguines surrounded her desk. They were so loud that she couldn't hear her clients on the phone. When she was in the ladies' room she was frequently interrupted by somebody hollering in to let her know she had a phone call. After a few weeks of working in this office, Leslie told her boss she had to quit. She couldn't handle the stress. Her boss was shocked as she and the other Popular Sanguines thought the fast pace and frequent emergencies kept the workplace fun and interesting. But, to a Perfect Melancholy the frenetic pace gave her anxiety attacks on the way to work.

As a Perfect Melancholy, Leslie would have needed a private office, or at least one with other quiet people, in order to stay. She needed others to respect her space and allow her to visit the ladies' room uninterrupted. As a part of her need for order, Leslie needed her pens to stay on her desk. In fact, many Perfect Melancholies resort to labeling their pens, scissors, and other desk equipment so when Popular Sanguines walk off with their supplies, they can find the culprits and regain possession. Leslie has since found employment in an office with more routine and less stress, and her Popular Sanguine boss has learned that although the idea of having someone organized around may be appealing, her office is not the place for Perfect Melancholy order and sensitivity.

If you have Perfect Melancholies in your workplace, be sensitive to their needs. Remember they don't make decisions hastily, so if you disagree, ask them for their reasoning. You'll probably find they are right. Allow them to have order in their work life. Give them space and realistic deadlines and don't change the rules. The Perfect Melancholy is a reliable, consistent worker who will be happiest with order and sensitivity.

CHAPTER 15

The Valuable Powerful Choleric: Appreciate Me

When you look at the entire puzzle of your workplace, you will see Powerful Cholerics are the ones who are consistently working. Work, or accomplishment, is one of the Powerful Choleric's emotional needs. If there is a birthday party at the office, Powerful Choleric will arrive late and leave early to allow for the maximum accomplishment in the workday. Others may chat from time to time, but Powerful Cholerics keep their productivity up.

While their other emotional need is appreciation for all they do, the other personalities may come to resent the Powerful Choleric's single-mindedness. It makes others look like they are slacking off and the Powerful Choleric's high production ruins the average for those who are not so driven.

Powerful Cholerics work harder than anyone else and therefore they produce more. Yet, others tend to resent their eagerness, and therefore Powerful Cholerics' work often goes unappreciated. Powerful Cholerics need accomplishment, but unlike Perfect Melancholies who can be at peace with themselves just knowing they've done a good job, Powerful Cholerics need appreciation for all their work. If they don't get the appreciation they need, they will work harder and accomplish more in hopes that others will notice. Their favorite line is, "After all I've done for you . . ."

Understanding Powerful Cholerics' need for production will help you in relating to them. Rather than trying to slow them down or suggest that they relax, praise them for their hard work. They will relax more when you comment on how well they are doing than when you ignore them or try to get them to slow down. That only makes them work harder in hopes you'll notice them.

As a secretary Lisa was amazing. She could type fast and flawlessly. She took on every task she was assigned as if her life depended on it. If Lisa said she would get something done, you didn't have to question her. You knew it was done and done right. However, as a Powerful Choleric Lisa never rested, and at times her constant activity made the others in the office nervous.

When there was an office social gathering, Lisa automatically took charge and began serving or cleaning, whichever was needed. Others would insist that she sit and rest, which made her nervous! It seemed like a no-win situation. Either Lisa made the others nervous or they made her jumpy. That was before they realized that Lisa was a Powerful Choleric.

Once her coworkers understood that Lisa needed to work, didn't like to rest, and needed praise for her work, they have settled into a happy medium. Lisa flutters about at social gatherings and does nearly all the work. The others relax and thank her profusely for her hard work and concern. In the office, the others have learned that just because Lisa never rests doesn't mean that they can't take breaks from time to time. When she is in one of her extreme Powerful Choleric modes, they stay out of her way. And when she comes up for air, the others have made a habit of telling her what a great job she is doing.

Powerful Cholerics will be your best and most reliable workers if their work is acknowledged.

If you are working for a Powerful Choleric, you'll fare better if you understand that his or her entire measuring stick of a person's worth is their productivity. A Powerful Choleric's time is valuable, as each minute represents something that can be accomplished. Don't keep a Powerful Choleric boss waiting, even if he or she is frequently late because other people's meetings don't really get underway for at least half an hour after they're scheduled.

Harold, a Powerful Choleric, hired Craig, a Peaceful Phlegmatic carpenter, to do some construction at his office on a Saturday while the office was closed. In a bad economy, Craig was grateful for the extra work. They had agreed that they would meet at the office at nine o'clock. Harold was there at five minutes to nine. He opened up the office and checked over the area that needed the work. Twenty minutes later Craig still wasn't there. Harold wrote a note stating that he had been there at nine o'clock, as planned, and that he couldn't wait any longer. He posted the note on the door and headed off to his next project. Later in the day Craig called begging Harold to go and open up the office so he could do the job. By then Harold was deep into a different project. He set a new time for the following weekend. Craig learned an important lesson for working with Powerful Cholerics—if you want the work, be on time.

If you have a Powerful Choleric boss, be sure to keep him or her apprised of all the work you are doing and have completed. You don't have to have a formal meeting to address your productivity. Just a casual comment in passing as to the progress you are making on a big project or the number of calls you've made will keep the Powerful Choleric aware of the fact that you are producing.

Mark is a Perfect Melancholy who carries out his work duties in a quiet and professional manner. His work is always done before it's needed, unless there are delays beyond his control. He was therefore shocked during his quarterly performance review. His Powerful Choleric boss had several complaints that he was sure just weren't true. The boss felt that several of Mark's projects weren't done on time, and he thought that there were things that had never been completed at all.

In fact, the project that was late was so because his boss had held it up. Mark had his part ready but he needed vital information from his boss before he could complete the project. By the time he got the needed information, the project was already late, and Mark did his best to make up for the lost time. In the end, the final project was late, and it appeared to be Mark's fault.

The other tasks that his boss thought were not completed had been done, but since the Powerful Choleric seeks attention for all of his accomplishments, he assumes that everyone else does also. As a Perfect Melancholy, Mark did not draw attention to each task he'd completed. Therefore his boss thought the items had been forgotten and not done.

How could these problems have been avoided with the knowledge that the Powerful Choleric places such a high premium on production? When a project is held up for a reason that is beyond your control, be sure that the Powerful Choleric is aware of the standing, what the problem is, and why the project is delayed. Point out what you have done already and what you are trying to do to correct the situation.

In Mark's case, when his boss decided to keep the project on his desk for some additional information, Mark should have reminded him that he had gotten his part done on time and that these new additions would postpone the project's completion. This way the Powerful Choleric boss would be aware of Mark's efforts and would make the decision as to whether or not to hold the project up for the new information. If he does choose to hold it up, he will clearly know that the delay is his choice and that Mark completed his part on time.

On the other tasks, if Mark had simply given his boss a memo or note stating that the tasks had been completed, there would be no question about his productivity.

Sarah is a strong Powerful Choleric married to a Peaceful Phlegmatic who took early retirement to devote more time to golf. She owns a children's clothing boutique and is more than slightly irked that he "does nothing" while she has to do "all the work." In reality, she doesn't have to do all the work, but as a typical Powerful Choleric she loves challenges and would feel guilty if she relaxed. As we discussed her marriage problems, she could see that they were really personality problems. She has learned to accept him as he is and be glad he doesn't complain about her compulsive need to be in control.

One day we analyzed her employees. She has three Powerful Cholerics who all want to be in control and who fight with each other for her attention and "favored nation status." They all tell her what the others aren't doing right and look for appreciation for every good work they've done. The Powerful Cholerics are all unhappy with the new Popular Sanguine employee who has had no training, doesn't do anything right, and yet sells more than they do. They are disgusted that she plays with the babies and furious when she pretends each grandmother is the baby's mother. "She's nothing but an act!" one Powerful Choleric cried out. But at the end of the day the act has paid off.

The one Perfect Melancholy is a hypochondriac who belabors her aches and pains each day. She is frequently unable to come to work because of ill health or an ill wind that stirs up the pollens and aggravates her allergies. When the Perfect Melancholy does check in, she tells Sarah that she doesn't really have to work as the others do. She is only working to give herself an excuse to get out of the house and is sacrificing her time to help Sarah out.

Sarah is grooming her one Peaceful Phlegmatic to become the manager because "she's the only one nobody hates." Her Powerful Choleric lawyer husband had left her without a cent and she has to work, much as she doesn't want to. She suppresses her true feelings most of the time, but occasionally her bitterness overwhelms her and her tears cause the Powerful Cholerics to proclaim her a weak woman. They have no intention of taking any orders from her, for if there's one thing a Powerful Choleric can't tolerate it's any form of weakness.

The high school girl who comes in part time is amused by the Popular Sanguine's game with the grandmothers, feels sorry for the lonely Peaceful Phlegmatic, avoids the Perfect Melancholy martyr, and says of the three Powerful Cholerics, "What do they think I am? The maid? They expect me to pick up after them."

Sarah's staff is functioning true to form, but at least she understands them and is able to meet their emotional needs. She applauds the Popular Sanguine's sales and personality, commiserates with the Perfect Melancholy's ailments, encourages the Peaceful Phlegmatic who doesn't feel she's worth "a plug nickel," and keeps the Powerful Choleric watchdogs from biting each other.

Powerful Cholerics need to know that you appreciate all their hard work. They often feel that they are carrying more than their share of the work load, which they may be. If those who work with Powerful Cholerics understand their needs for appreciation and achievement, and praise them, they will be much more pleasant in the workplace.

CHAPTER 16

The Valuable Peaceful Phlegmatic:
Respect Me

Just like Peaceful Phlegmatics' visible and various pieces of the Puzzle, their valuable pieces are not obvious to the casual observer. Peaceful Phlegmatics' emotional need is for respect and feelings of self-worth. Because of their quiet and complacent nature, Peaceful Phlegmatics appear to be content wherever they are and with whatever is going on. That appearance is exactly what gives them such a need for respect and feelings of self-worth.

Popular Sanguines gauge people by how fun and exciting they are. Since Peaceful Phlegmatics don't naturally create fun and excitement, Popular Sanguines tend not to value Peaceful Phlegmatics.

Perfect Melancholies appreciate people who have life organized and are deep and thoughtful. Since Peaceful Phlegmatics tend to float through life and may never boast about having it all together, Perfect Melancholies may not respect Peaceful Phlegmatics.

Powerful Cholerics judge all of life by production, and since Peaceful Phlegmatics would rather rest than work, they are often made to feel worthless by Powerful Cholerics.

A life of being overlooked and undervalued has created a deep longing for respect and feelings of self-worth in Peaceful Phlegmatics. Yet, whomever they turn to, Peaceful Phlegmatics are left feeling like Rodney Dangerfield. They get no respect!

Brian is a Peaceful Phlegmatic who works in his father's manufacturing business. His father is a driven Powerful Choleric who retired for a short time but couldn't stand the lack of production. At age seventy he bought a struggling company and with his Powerful Choleric personality, he turned it into a major player in its industry. Brian handles the trade shows and manages the sales, yet he never does well enough for his father's praise. Brian married Janice when he was twenty three. He says that Janice, a Popular Sanguine, was the first person to believe in him. Since they have been married, Brian has blossomed. His father still doesn't give him any credit for the good job he does, but his wife encourages him and has made him feel special.

If you work with Peaceful Phlegmatics be sure to notice what they do and how well they do it. For Brian one of the most frustrating things is how little value his father places on his ideas. Rather than acknowledging any of Brian's ideas that may have some merit or explaining why they aren't feasible, Brian's dad quickly dismisses them and squelches any further creativity.

To avoid this in your workplace, listen when Peaceful Phlegmatics speak. As they may be quieter than some of the others, you may have to make an effort to actually hear them. They may share their ideas more slowly, but don't jump in and finish their thoughts. Wait for some signal that they have completed their sentence. That, in itself, will indicate that you care to Peaceful Phlegmatics. Once you have heard their ideas, repeat them in your own words so they know that you really heard them. Thank them for their creativity or thoughtfulness. Then, either act upon their idea or explain why it is a great idea but you don't think it will work right now. The combination of discussing the idea and then either acting upon the plan or explaining why it won't work is an investment in them that shows you respect their thinking. This can greatly improve the relationship. Most Peaceful Phlegmatics have gone through life feeling that no one ever listens to them. If you listen, you will have a friend for life.

Ruth is a Peaceful Phlegmatic who has her life all figured out. For twenty years, she has worked as a nurse in a nursing home. She works from midnight until eight in the morning. She goes home and sleeps while the kids are in school and is awake to spend the afternoon with them.

As a Peaceful Phlegmatic, she loves her job because she works alone and isn't bothered by any of the other nurses or support staff. All she has to do is make rounds and give medication. She has a lot of time to herself and gets a lot of reading done. Her coworkers applaud her faithfulness. She is sure and steady, and they never have to worry if Ruth will be there to replace them at midnight. The morning shift knows that Ruth will do what she was supposed to, and everything will be ready for them when they arrive.

No one wants her shift, so everyone is very appreciative of what Ruth does. In turn, Ruth gets her needs met through her work. She has the time to herself that she loves and gets the support and respect that nourish her emotionally. As a Peaceful Phlegmatic, Ruth is a very valuable piece of the Puzzle, and the rest of the team treats her as such!

When the emotional needs of Peaceful Phlegmatics are met, they will be a faithful and dependable part of the overall picture in your workplace.

Josh started working for a health food company as someone who could help out in a variety of ways. As a Peaceful Phlegmatic, Josh agreeably took on whatever tasks needed to be done. As the company grew, Josh grew with it. After a few years, he became the warehouse manager. Josh created systems for shipping and record keeping as the need arose. He functioned smoothly, and orders always got out on time. If there was ever a problem with a lost shipment, people on the other end always appreciated the calm way Josh handled the situation. He never got angry with them, and they always knew Josh would take care of the problem.

As the company continued to grow, his haven was interrupted one day. Josh needed some part-time help in the warehouse. They sent in one of the young women from another department. Lucy was a Powerful Choleric who loved computers. As Josh was trying to teach her all the systems for getting the orders filled and shipped out, Lucy immediately saw many ways to improve the process. With complete disregard for Josh's systems or reasoning, Lucy blurted out several things that would make the functioning more efficient. Josh was hurt. He had spent years creating his own world that functioned smoothly. Everyone was happy with the end product. Although Lucy was probably right, it wasn't the best way to work with a Peaceful Phlegmatic. The relationship got off on the wrong foot, and it took a long time for the initial shock to wear off.

Debbie is a Super Powerful Choleric businesswoman, who by sheer guts and determination rose to a controlling position over teams of men. She assigned each group where to go and what to do. She was too busy achieving to have a social life. As she says, "I ran over everyone in my path." In her thirties she began to wish she had a normal life and she prayed that she would find a husband. Since she is practical even in prayer, she asked the Lord to bring her a man with a station wagon. It would save her from going out to buy one. Along came Bill in a station wagon, and it was love at first sight. Since Debbie is Super Powerful Choleric, you can guess that Bill is Super Peaceful Phlegmatic.

Debbie immediately put Bill into her business, unwisely gave him a controlling position, and let her Powerful Choleric underlings pick on him. She felt he'd learn faster if she just threw him into the pit with the corporate wolves.

Debbie didn't understand that passive Bill hated confrontation, wilted under criticism, and had come out of a childhood of rejection. As she saw what she considered failure on his part, she lost respect for him, demoted him, and took control once again. This action triggered his feelings of low self-worth and rejection, and he withdrew from Debbie and the business.

"He seemed afraid of success," Debbie explained. As she began to "play the man" in their relationship, they both lost interest in sex and showed little emotional response to each other.

This marriage was headed toward disaster until Debbie came to a Personality Plus seminar and began to understand Bill's emotional needs. Until then she had judged everyone by her standards—either work hard or get out. She began to realize that with her driving nature she needed a restful husband who could be a calming influence on her life. She needed the quiet port in her excitingly turbulent times of tension. She had to stop trying to change her husband into a Powerful Choleric like her. She had to release him from functioning in his weaknesses and let him work where he could excel. That was clearly not under her control.

As she began to understand his personality, Debbie suggested he go back to his own career where people admired his patience and pleasant personality. Once they were no longer working together, Debbie and Bill rebuilt their relationship. He was happy to help her with dinner preparations and listen to the trials she'd had with the dummies at work—now that he wasn't one of them. She was glad to come home to a peaceful man who relaxed her as she walked in the front door.

Debbie told me that understanding the Personality Puzzle saved her marriage, gave her a perspective of how the men at work looked at her, and caused her to tone down her authoritative manner. She also desired to meet her Peaceful Phlegmatic husband's emotional needs. In her words, "I have it etched in my brain, 'make him feel worthy.'"

If you work with Peaceful Phlegmatics, remember that they probably grew up feeling more overlooked and less talented than others. You can make work their favorite place by giving them respect and feelings of self-worth. Peaceful Phlegmatics can be the most valuable piece of the Puzzle. Be sure to let them know how valuable they are!

CHAPTER 17

Putting the Pieces Together

Whatever kind of business you are in, an understanding of the Personality Puzzle will enable you to get along with others and work effectively together. All pieces have a place in the Puzzle and when you can find where they fit, everyone will be happy. The following discussion of various kinds of businesses carries lessons that are applicable in other kinds.

Personalities in the Restaurant Business

We were in the restaurant business for twenty years, and we learned how important it was to put the pieces of the Personality Puzzle where they belong. We found that the combination of Popular Sanguines and Powerful Cholerics made the best waitresses. The Popular Sanguines tended to talk too much and not get to all their customers, and the Powerful Cholerics got the people waited on quickly but too brusquely. If we could find the Popular Sanguine personality with the Powerful Choleric desire to work, we had outstanding waitresses. Some Perfect Melancholies were very good on the details of waitressing, seeing that everyone was served properly, graciously, and on time. The problem came when they had a bad day, and their depression kept them from even saying hello to the customers. Peaceful Phlegmatics never seemed to care quite enough to hurry during the busy lunch time, but we could use them effectively on the slower hours.

Popular Sanguines combined with the Powerful Cholerics were also the best for the cash desk, hostess job. They could be pleasant and conversant and yet remember to keep their minds and eyes on the money. We had both Perfect Melancholy and Peaceful Phlegmatic office workers who did well when properly motivated.

Our best short-order cooks were always Powerful Cholerics who loved the pressure of the job and produced miraculously under duress. Peaceful

Phlegmatics were good cooks, not getting rattled when things got hectic, and they could always calm down upset customers.

One Perfect Melancholy manager did very well in seeing that all the details were carried out correctly, and she also had compassion for the problems the waitresses always seemed to have in their personal lives.

By analyzing the temperament of the prospective employees, we were able to put the proper people in the right spots and produce harmonious results.

Personalities in the Medical Field

Florence frequently speaks at a variety of medical conventions. She starts with a tongue-in-cheek observation of the medical Personality Puzzle that goes like the following. But the principle will hold true for people in any job or industry.

Popular Sanguine doctors become pediatricians so they can play with the children and not have to grow up. They can fill their waiting rooms with teddy bears and tiny trucks and decorate the walls with cheerful posters of Minnie Mouse. They can have their assistants dress in colorful costumes and can make coming to the doctor an exciting experience for children. As they give out helium balloons to those little ones who didn't cry when stabbed with the needle, they can be heard to say, "Wasn't this fun!"

Powerful Choleric doctors can't bear to work under others, especially others who are incompetent. Wasn't that endless residency degrading enough? They soon tire of controlling only the lives and destinies of their patients and have the uncontrollable urge to dictate to fellow physicians. To do this they start clinics and bring on Peaceful Phlegmatics who don't want the responsibility of running an office. Initially this seems to be a positive blending of the best in opposite personalities. It works fine until the day when the Powerful Choleric spouse of a Peaceful Phlegmatic physician walks in to find out why his or her spouse is not getting a fair share of the profits.

Perfect Melancholies often become surgeons. When you think of it would you want a Popular Sanguine operating on your brain? "Oh my, isn't this cute?" Perfect Melancholies are perfectionists, give endless thought to what they are doing, and above all, don't want to make any mistakes. Isn't that the kind of person you want cutting into you?

Perfect Melancholies also become psychiatrists and spend the rest of their lives in constant self-analysis. What other personalities would want to study that long, that hard, and that deep on depressive topics only to end up listening to perpetual bad news daily and salvaging suicidal patients from the brink of disaster?

Peaceful Phlegmatics often become radiologists taking harmless pictures and letting someone else bear the responsibility of deciding what to do with the results. Many Peaceful Phlegmatics become dentists. Among teeth, they are not apt to be in life and death situations. They can go quietly about their business, and they don't care if people don't like them.

In reality there are definite differences in the physicians' personalities. If you are a nurse working with residents, there are certain basics that will help you. Keep in mind that whatever position you're in, in health care or any other industry, these principles will apply.

To deal with the controlling Powerful Choleric resident, it is best never to "tell" them anything. Instead ask them what they think about the situation. Agree with them if possible. Then add another thought that will make their plan even better. Remember they need affirmation and loyalty, and they will never forgive you if you embarrass them or plot a mini-mutiny. As residents they are a little insecure way inside, but they don't want anyone to know that, so they tend to be very defensive if pushed. They become angry if exposed as appearing weak. To obtain the best results praise their good works, applaud their long and tireless hours on the job, and encourage them to initiate all necessary changes. At first, they can't believe the nurses want to work with them and not against them. But if you work hard and don't cross them up they will ultimately see that you are on their team.

In dealing with the Perfect Melancholy, residents realize their need for perfection and support. Before approaching them with a problem be sure you have your facts straight, your data ready to present, and your mind in order. Nothing frustrates Perfect Melancholies more than an unprepared Popular Sanguine who has bright, creative thoughts but no vague idea of how to implement them. New Perfect Melancholy residents are often overwhelmed by the speed and arrogance of Powerful Cholerics, and they are apt to get depressed and moody. They need sensitive support. They will not make friends quickly so be patient. Their moods will be as variable as the weather so try to sense their highs and lows before tossing off a thoughtless comment that they may hear as a condemnation.

Peaceful Phlegmatic residents are the easiest to handle as they want any assistance possible to keep them out of trouble. Anything you can do to make them look good and any steps you can take to save them effort will be deeply appreciated. They aren't trying to win points or bring attention on themselves, so they are the easiest to please.

Peaceful Phlegmatics are always hesitant to step in and make quick decisions. They are willing to let others bear responsibility. They don't enjoy the long hours, have low motivation, and can hardly wait to get through the rotations that keep throwing them into situations where they'll be tested. Peaceful Phlegmatics are easygoing, pleasant, inoffensive. They welcome your suggestions, are thrilled when you do their work, and agree with just about anything.

Popular Sanguine residents hope this program will be fun and exciting and know from the start that everyone will love them. They soon find the sheer scope of what is expected of them is "too much like work." In dealing with the Popular Sanguines, remember that they don't stay in one spot for long. You need to pin them down quickly before they disappear. Many Popular Sanguines can't remember where they left the medical charts with all the patients' private information, and sometimes they don't even know if this patient is theirs. They will love you if you can keep track of their possessions, hand them what they need at the right time and not point out where they left things or embarrass them in front of people. Help them get organized, make them look good, laugh at their stories, and you will be their friend for life—unless they forget who you are tomorrow.

In every business, an understanding of the Personality Puzzle can smooth out the rough spots. Be thinking about your workplace. How can you use this knowledge to improve your business situation?

Personalities in Network Marketing

Couples in network marketing groups are often taught that the man always presents the plan and keeps track of the orders and finances. The woman socializes at meetings, fills and delivers the orders, and does all the follow-up on the phone. After reading *Personality Plus,* one group began to train their people to use their personality strengths regardless of their gender. Popular Sanguines, male or female, greet new people and make them feel wanted. They start meetings with a light touch and then turn the business over to the Perfect Melancholy who understands the finances. In the Powerful Choleric/Peaceful Phlegmatic couple, the Powerful Choleric likes to do the presenting. But it is important to have the Peaceful Phlegmatic share in a sincere low-pressure manner about the personal benefits of the business. Whichever person is better at money matters should keep the books. And when both partners have other jobs they should share the follow-up calls and deliveries. We have found with these simple understandings that the conflict caused by "that's the woman's job" has been relieved.

Since network marketing is often an extra occupation, it is especially important to use the Personality Puzzle as a tool. As we have closely observed many different network groups we have found that the couples who make it to the top are functioning cooperatively with each other and have an understanding of their individual personalities. Those who are working in their weaknesses or without the Personality Puzzle as a tool often end up with marriage problems and business failure. There are many circumstances we can't control in life, but we can use our knowledge of the Personality Puzzle to keep us functioning in our strengths and not slogging along in our weaknesses.

Judy wrote about how her husband fit the personality pieces together in his business.

After reading *Personality Plus* and hearing Florence speak on several occasions, I suggested to my husband, Mark, that he consider applying some of the principles we had learned to his growing multilevel marketing business. Mark already had laid the groundwork for building his organization. He gave his recruits plenty of sponsor support, educated them on company products, and kept the lines of communication open. A Powerful Choleric himself, Mark was driven to succeed. The challenge of beating others, coupled with the desire to make money, was all it took to motivate him. Yet it wasn't so for some others in his group. . . .

After meeting with each training representative in his region, accompanying them on their sales and recruiting presentations, and watching them interact in a group atmosphere, Mark made several deductions. First he found that the Perfect Melancholies make great teachers. They have the ability to educate others on company programs, substantiate their claims with facts and figures, and also clearly explain the benefits of the multilevel marketing system to the average consumer. These qualities were essential to building a large, successful multilevel organization. However, Perfect Melancholies aren't "pie in the sky" types. They want pay in proportion to effort and cannot stand dead time. They are intrigued by the magic of compound interest, the multiplication factor characteristic of multilevel marketing and the residual income it offers. They are motivated by special promotions where they can win savings bonds, electronic personal organizers, scientific calculators, and stereo systems with added features and components and books of complicated instructions.

Second, Mark learned that the Peaceful Phlegmatics worked as much for appreciation as they did for money. They exhibited the need for value and acceptance more than the other personality types and were concerned that those they recruited into the business made just as much money, even more than they did. Peaceful Phlegmatics took good care of their customers and helped all, regardless of how much product they bought or distributed. Peaceful Phlegmatics also were the most difficult to motivate. While the Perfect Melancholy wants pay in proportion to effort, the Peaceful Phlegmatic wants greater pay with less work. This personality type loves to relax, therefore vacations without much activity (cruises, a weekend at a luxury hotel, etc.) appeal to them. In addition, Peaceful Phlegmatics enjoy dinner-for-two, massages, and makeovers. Probably the one thing that keeps Peaceful Phlegmatics motivated to continue building a multilevel marketing organization is the fact that one day they will be getting paid without ever having to get out of bed!

Opposite of the Peaceful Phlegmatic, the Powerful Choleric is naturally driven to succeed. Mark had little difficulty getting this group to work; they were always moving ahead, reaching for the next level and looking for leadership opportunities. Their long-term motivation comes from the excitement of being in a multilevel program. Powerful Cholerics win most contests anyway but are more concerned with the bonus percentages being paid out than actually winning a prize. They're motivated by opportunity and money and if the right opportunity comes along, stay out of their way!

Finally, Mark was confronted with the Popular Sanguine, the "natural" salesperson. While the other personality types don't enjoy calling on strangers and talking them into something they don't need or want, the Popular Sanguine doesn't know a stranger and doesn't even "sell" anything. Many people purchase products from or are recruited by

Popular Sanguines because they're fun to be around and they just take others along for the ride. Popular Sanguines love parties in their honor, large trophies, funny gadgets, and exciting trips with lots of activities, sporting events, and team participation. Both the Popular Sanguines and the Powerful Cholerics love awards ceremonies and having their name in company newsletters and bulletins.

If, by chance, Mark found himself having a difficult time motivating an individual, he'd apply the same principles to motivate the spouse, then use him or her to encourage the partner to produce. It only took a few shopping sprees awarded to enthusiastic spouses to greatly increase production in Mark's region and win him the promotion he so desperately wanted.

Within six months after implementing some of these ideas, Mark's organization was doing two to three times the production it previously had done. Applying what he had learned from Florence's materials and, with a little experimentation of his own, Mark was well on his way to becoming one of the top managers in the state.

As Mark did, you can learn to piece the personalities in your workplace together.

Personalities in the Office

One man who came to one of our seminars on the temperaments went back to his office and took a look at his problems. He was a Powerful Choleric, and he wanted everything to be done quickly and well. He had, unfortunately, put people in certain jobs because they had happened to arrive looking for work on the day he needed a body. Many had fallen into positions in which they were unfit and uncomfortable.

He pulled the Popular Sanguines out of the back offices where they were bored and doing poorly at the books and made them into receptionists and salespeople. He assigned the Perfect Melancholies to see that all the book work was done properly by the Peaceful Phlegmatics, and he put his one other Powerful Choleric in charge of the whole office, freeing his own time up for creative thinking.

Remember: Popular Sanguines do well in situations where contact with people is important. They are good on the phone, out front, as receptionists, in sales, creating new ideas, and in personnel. Don't expect them to balance the books. Popular Sanguines feel that if the columns come out to within a few dollars that is close enough. They are not good on details, figures, and the right time, but they will keep people happy.

Remember: Powerful Cholerics are goal oriented. If you can provide challenges and rewards, you will keep them moving and making progress. They do well in charge of anything as long as you can impress upon them how important it is to get along with others. A combination of the Popular Sanguine and the Powerful Choleric with a pleasant personality and purposeful desire is an ideal combination for leadership.

Remember: Perfect Melancholies work best unencumbered by people. They keep their desks in order, balance their books, write their letters neatly, and always show up for work on time. You can count on them to perform to the best of their ability at all times if you can keep their working conditions agreeable. They do well on all details, on long-range planning, and will be loyal to you for life if treated respectfully.

Remember: Peaceful Phlegmatics can be great workers if you can motivate them properly. They do well in a structured environment where their work is spelled out clearly and they can see what they have to do and check it off. Left on their own, they may waste time. They don't do well when they are left to function when they feel like it. The time just never seems to be right, and they tend to procrastinate. They are excellent at mediating office problems as they can see both sides objectively.

Personalities in Teaching

It is helpful, when dealing with many young pupils, to understand which personality type you can count on and for what. Young Popular Sanguines may be discipline problems who want to talk more than work. But they can be motivated to keep quiet when you show them how much that would mean to you. They always want to be liked by others, and appealing to their desire to please will bring them into line. They are always good at oral reports, and they love to be leaders of groups where some original thinking has to be done. Since they are undisciplined, they need to be frequently reminded about due dates for large projects. They profit from having a typed list of what is expected of them—if they don't lose the list.

Little Powerful Cholerics are usually motivated to get things done on time and well. They sometimes get into trouble when they don't have enough to do and finish before the others. Both of us had teachers who reported that if they could only keep us busy we were all right. But the minute we finished ahead of the others, we would start to talk and disturb the rest of the class.

Melancholies love involved projects and details, and they will work quietly to achieve the goal. Remember that they'll be easily hurt by the teacher or other pupils who say things that offend them. These problems should be dealt with quickly before the pupil goes into a depression.

Peaceful Phlegmatics never really jump into anything with great enthusiasm, so don't be disturbed if they put a wet blanket on your grand plan for the year. They will probably work at a big project in their own time, and they may even get to like the project. You can be sure they will behave well, won't stir up trouble with the others, and will be consistently pleasant.

A nursery school teacher came to one of our seminars, and she went back with a new perspective on her little pupils. She called to report that she could identify their temperaments. Even these young ones reacted true to form. She was a Powerful Choleric herself, and she had never understood why the whole group did not do just what she instructed. After being exposed to the Personality Puzzle, she saw that it was Popular Sanguines who babbled on all day and just wanted to play. They hated to be kept in their chairs, and they got up and ran around as soon as she looked the other way. The little Powerful Cholerics did their work well, got through quickly, and then started bossing the others around and making fun of them because they were slow. They were happiest when the teacher left them in charge of the class for a few minutes, sent them to the office on errands, and let them run all of the games at recess.

While the Powerful Cholerics charged in full of pep each morning, the Perfect Melancholies and Peaceful Phlegmatics came in less eagerly. A Perfect Melancholy in a good mood would get right down to work. They liked schedules. She said she appreciated the Perfect Melancholies because they tried not to cause her any trouble. They were proud when they finished, but they got discouraged if they could not get everything done that they had been assigned.

Peaceful Phlegmatics were very agreeable and moved when the teacher said to move. Their minds seemed to drift from their work, and they were most happy when she would let them sit in the corner and build with blocks all day. She said that her understanding of the temperaments made each day a colorful experience and she no longer worried over why each child did not see things exactly her way.

A high school teacher, Larry, was so excited over the *Personality Plus* material that he took it back to his classes and tested each group. The teenagers were fascinated with the self-analysis. And using it, he was able to anticipate the needs of each class far better than he had before. Soon other pupils wanted to take the Personality Profile to find out about themselves. And then other teachers wanted to know what he was doing that had the teens so eager to go to his class. After two successful years working with the students, he began classes to train the other teachers on the practical use of the temperaments. Not only has this helped pupil/teacher and pupil/pupil relationships, but the teachers now understand each other better. There is a harmony and a humor in the school which has been rewarding.

CHAPTER 18

Advertising and Selling by the Personality Puzzle

Whatever your business is, there is apt to be a time when you need to do some type of advertising. Earlier in *Personality Puzzle* we talked about various kinds of advertising that appeal to the different pieces of the Personality Puzzle. In putting the pieces together in your workplace, the following guidelines will help you.

Many small companies need advertising to sell their products or services. Yet no one knows how to create an ad that will attract the right people. Now that you understand the Personality Puzzle you will be better able to target your correct audience.

The first question to ask yourself is: What personality do I want to attract? If we don't ask this question we tend to create advertising out of our own personality and not into the personality of the customer. Even major advertising agencies make mistakes in the directions they take. "It's so hard," says Bill D'Ambrosia of DMB&B, an ad agency. "You have to please so many people. If you hit .200, if you get two out of ten ads through that you love, you're doing great" (*USA Today,* 31 Oct. 1991).

Perhaps we can do better than batting .200. Perhaps we can hit the target more often than the agencies if we use the Personality Puzzle as our guide. Is our product or service something fun that will appeal to Popular Sanguines? Something practical that will speed up activity for Powerful Cholerics? Something detailed that will facilitate organization for Perfect Melancholies? Something soothing that will make the pains of life easier for Peaceful Phlegmatics? Once you decide what people you wish to attract, then you can create ads that will draw them and not waste money scattering seeds on the wrong soil.

Ads for Popular Sanguines

To appeal to Popular Sanguines, use words like *fun* and *thrilling*. Grandmother Popular Sanguines, eager for praise, will buy any toys or trinkets that seem exciting. They will outdo the other side of the family, even if they have to spend the next year paying it off. Any nonessential trendy item that will make the purchaser feel ahead of the crowd or a part of the jet set should be pitched to the Popular Sanguine.

Eliminate paragraphs of fine print or columns of statistics and go for the big picture, the splash, the color, the cartoons. Now that you know Popular Sanguines are out for fun, even if you aren't one yourself, imagine what would appeal to an adult whose desires are still childlike.

Ads for Powerful Cholerics

Bold letters, a clear message, the promise of power, speed, and control, are features that attract the practical Powerful Choleric mind. Powerful Cholerics don't wish to waste time reading details, and they turn from childish games. Let's get on with life and get the work done. Airline magazines are full of ads directed toward Powerful Cholerics. Seminars on how to win by intimidation, hotels where you can spread your papers out and still have room to get into bed, travel bargains for those with the right credit cards, briefcases with wheels and retractable handles, compartmentalized suitcases that duplicate your dresser at home, and cellular phones that allow you to continue business during lunch all appeal to Powerful Cholerics.

If you are directing your promotion to the Powerful Choleric keep it sharp, clear, and uncluttered. And always show what it can do to save them time right *now!*

Ads for Perfect Melancholies

Perfect Melancholies are drawn to ads that appeal to the mind: definitions, statistics, charts, graphs, and columns. They will read the fine print and meditate over the copy. Urgency doesn't appeal to them as they intend to weigh over all the possibilities and comparison shop before making a purchase. They love new organizational tools such as calendars and hour-by-hour schedules, purpose pages, and long-range goal-setting pages. Fred enjoys reading about new pens, flashlights, and retractable measuring tapes.

If you have items to promote that fit the Perfect Melancholy's love of details and gadgets, don't fluff up the ad with daisies and pink bunnies.

These cute trimmings, while appealing to Popular Sanguines, communicate to the Perfect Melancholy that what you have to offer is trivial and of little consequence.

Ads for Peaceful Phlegmatics

Will what you are selling save time and conserve energy? Will it solve problems and eliminate conflict? Will it cure headaches and nervous allergies? Will it be comfortable to wear or soft to lie on? Will it cook in a microwave or boil in a little plastic pouch? These are the products and offers that appeal to Peaceful Phlegmatics. They enjoy dry humor and puns and can be attracted by cartoons and offers of low-energy fun. They like fishing because it's called a sport and yet you don't have to work at it. You can just sit in a boat with some other semi-comatose friends and wait for the fish to come along and activate the process.

If you have goods that make life easier or services that really serve, you will want to promote them to the Peaceful Phlegmatic in a simple way that won't look too much like work.

Some of you may say "Well I want to hit everyone." Don't try so hard to hit everyone that you hit no one, but use the tool of the Personality Puzzle to measure your thrust and bring focus to your direction. Use vocabulary words that appeal to the personality you have in mind. For example:

Sanguine

- fun-filled
- exciting and romantic
- hilarious
- free prizes
- gift included
- lavishly decorated

Choleric

- challenging and powerful
- thrilling
- practical
- quick and active
- bold and dramatic
- increases productivity

Phlegmatic

- easy and simple
- user friendly
- timesaving
- effortless
- relaxing
- soothing

Melancholy

- organized and systemized
- intellectual
- detailed
- sensitive
- automatic
- perfectly engineered

How could we create an ad for this book? Here's an ad for this book. Imagine a colorful brochure. The front cover says: "This practical book will increase your productivity, help you organize your life, make you more relaxed at work, and even entertain you." Note that no one type is going to be attracted by all the benefits of this book. But there's something in that headline for everyone.

Underneath the headline are four pictures. One shows a group of people excitedly talking around the watercooler. They're dressed in bright colors and all of them are gesturing with their hands and arms. You can almost hear them saying, "I laughed so hard when I read the section on my type. They sure pegged me. But, you know, I've really loved coming to work lately. It seems like so much more fun."

Another shows a take-charge type sitting behind a desk. There's a chart behind him with lines indicating increased production in blue and increased sales in black. Both lines are going up at a steep angle. You can almost hear him say, "I have gotten bold and dramatic results by implementing the ideas in this book. And, you know, even though people are working harder, it seems they're more appreciative of me." Uh huh!

Another picture shows a woman in a practical blue dress. Her office is as meticulous as her person. She's sitting at her desk, working at a computer. No one is interrupting her, and you can tell by the look on her face that she's thinking what a relief it is that those other people are leaving her alone to get her work done.

The final picture shows a casually dressed man with his feet up on the desk. He seems to be daydreaming, but there's quite a large stack of papers in his out box. He's thinking to himself, "It's so much easier to get things done now that my boss isn't nagging me constantly. All I have to do is let her know that I'm making progress and she seems not to care that I don't get here on the stroke of 9:00."

Inside the brochure is a detailed list of the contents of the book, to appeal to Powerful Cholerics and Perfect Melancholies. Some of the words are bold and dramatic. And some of them are intellectual and detailed. But on another page are more pictures of happy people working together. You just know they're having fun. The words on this page are brief and in bold colors: exciting, learn how to make your coworkers like you, work can be fun. And on yet another page is a picture of an empty desk. The sign on it says "Gone Fishing." Underneath, the copy reads: I learned so much about working from my own strength and interacting with my colleagues that I can get my work done and take time off.

You get the idea. Some products or services will have a benefit for each of the types. But those benefits will always be different. Know which facet of your product or service appeals to which type and use that knowledge in your advertising. Not only can you design brochures or ads highlighting various benefits, you can design different ads for the same product or service but targeted to different types. You can also place those ads in media that will be more likely to be read or seen by each personality type. There's no sense placing an ad aimed at Popular Sanguines in an accountants' trade journal. But you might advertise the same product or service in a different way in the Sunday newspaper.

Each personality has a place in the puzzle of your workplace, whether they are your customers or clients or coworkers.

Want Ads for Different Personalities

Understanding the Personality Puzzle is not only helpful in advertising to different kinds of people but also in looking *for* different types to complete your puzzle. When you wish to place a want ad for new personnel, you can draw certain personalities according to what you present in the ad.

Remember there is no person who has all strengths and no weaknesses so decide what type of person is best for the opening you have and write your ad to fit the type. Why waste time training mistakes?

If you are looking for a Popular Sanguine, up-front person who will relate well to people, then you should use words in the ad like: fun, enjoyable, exciting, never monotonous, work with congenial people. Offer: opportunity to meet people, travel, colorful environment, variety of jobs, constant activity, flexible schedule, talk on the phone, personal contact with fascinating people.

If you want a Powerful Choleric take-charge person to run your office or control situations, use words like: self-starter, dynamic personality, aggressive. Offer: opportunity for quick advancement, unusual challenges, fast-growing company, autonomous position, never dull, be your own boss.

If you want a Perfect Melancholy to be the organized detail-conscious person, use words like: meticulous, attention to detail, precise, complete projects on time, deep-thinker, creative, serious about business. Offer:

uninterrupted work, private office, state-of-the-art equipment, and intellectual atmosphere.

If you want a calm, balanced Peaceful Phlegmatic who will never cause trouble, use words like: mediator, get along with people, casual attire, valued member of team. Offer: a relaxed atmosphere, low-pressure job, established routine, flexibility, and pleasant surroundings.

Selling to Different Personalities

No matter what you are selling—clothes, houses, cars, soap, ideas, or workshops—you need to remember a key principle: Sell into their personality, not out of yours. The same principle holds true if you are sharing your faith. Since you have the ability to spot a person's temperament by observing their clothes and conversation, you have the upper hand in approaching anyone and no longer need to take your chances with the law of averages.

Once you spot a chatty, optimistic Popular Sanguine looking for color, creativity, and comedy, you know how to laugh at their stories and make your product sound like fun. If you're selling clothing, let them know its the latest thing. They love to be current. Show the women flowers, ruffles, sequins, and anything that wiggles like fringes. For men, display loud ties that would make a Perfect Melancholy blush and sports coats that are colorful and stylish. If you're selling cars, show them the bright colors, sliding sun roof, and excessive chrome trim. If you're showing a house, point out how it's designed for lavish parties, how a coat of mauve paint will turn the powder room into a jewel box, and how thrilled their friends will be to know the mayor lives down the street.

If you're promoting network marketing, show them how, in just a few hours work a week, they can get all their soap free, have money left over to spend on exciting extras, and win trips to Hawaii.

Just the opposite is the Perfect Melancholy who will not be impressed with surface satire or garish glitz. Appeal to them through their minds and express that you can sense their depth and compassion for others. Don't exaggerate or oversell. Just be serious and sincere.

If you are selling clothes, point out quality not quantity. Help them see how to build a mix and match ensemble on basic black with some simple accessories. Do not suggest wild jungle prints or marabou around the hemline. Save these for Popular Sanguines.

If you are selling houses, don't take the Perfect Melancholy to a place that has poor workmanship or is on a busy street. One agent told me that when she shows houses on a new tract she brings the Popular Sanguine to the homes right near the entrance of the development or by the pool where they can see everyone that comes and goes. The Perfect Melancholies she takes to the back away from the noise and action, preferably looking out on open fields or a brook. Perfect Melancholies will want to measure and meditate so don't hurry them along.

If you sell cars, the Perfect Melancholy will want to examine all the details, look through the owner's manual, and read through the fine print in the contract. Be prepared with statistics.

In network marketing, Perfect Melancholies aren't an easy sell, as they are suspicious of any "get-rich-quick scheme." They will not respond to hype and will listen better in a quiet place with one-on-one attention. They will study the plan and ask you questions you were never asked before. Don't make up answers, but tell them you'll get right back to them as soon as you check. And then be sure to do it, or they will cancel you out. Emphasize long-range profit and building for the future instead of trips, parties, and prizes.

When selling anything to Powerful Cholerics, remember that they want to know the bottom line quickly as they have no time to waste. In clothing, they want things that are practical, will wear well, and will give the look of success. They don't want gimmicks or fluff, but they want fabric that moves easily, stretches, and is not constricting.

Powerful Cholerics usually make the decisions on major items, such as houses and cars. They can analyze quickly, sift the good from the bad, and instinctively know what to choose. While Popular Sanguines talk about it and Perfect Melancholies think about it, Powerful Cholerics act on it. They want a house that is located near their work or a freeway access. They choose sturdiness over style and want a floor plan that will work for the family.

In cars, they are more apt to be impressed by the horsepower and miles-per-gallon than by the texture of the upholstery. They love to bargain and will push until they get the best price. They will do quick comparison shopping and buy from the person who comes down on price the most, even if they don't like the color. Remember they are after control in every phase of life, so help them to think they have taken charge and won.

If you are promoting network marketing, Powerful Cholerics are your best bet. They are the only personality who can work two or three jobs and keep going. They are usually business minded and will be able to grasp your circles and charts without lengthy explanation. Be sure you "know your stuff" when sharing your plan, or they may challenge you and take over the meeting or consider you a lightweight and leave quickly. They have to make every moment count.

In selling to Peaceful Phlegmatics, remember that they hate pushy people. People have tried to con them all their lives, and they sense insincerity and hype quite quickly. While they appear passive and will nod affirmation at your presentation, underneath they have that stubborn will of iron that will only be pulled so far before it rebels. Talking gently, encouraging them to take their time, and letting them know you are trying to help them, not sell them, will relax them and allow them to open their minds to your product.

Clothing is not important to the Peaceful Phlegmatic. They just don't care that much. They want to be well-dressed, but they don't have a passion for anything in particular. They need to be reassured that the item enhances their looks, and because they are insecure you need to give them confidence that this is the current fashion and is right for them personally. Ask about their occupation, chat with them in a low-key voice, and let them take their time and think it over. Often Peaceful Phlegmatic women bring a Powerful Choleric friend along who will take over for you and sell what they deem is right. Peaceful Phlegmatic men are often accompanied by a Powerful Choleric wife who will make your job unnecessary.

It is rare that a Peaceful Phlegmatic will make the final decision on a house without family support. But often a Powerful Choleric mate will send them out to narrow the prospects down. Peaceful Phlegmatics will say things like, "My husband hates stairs." Or, "He can't stand flowered wallpaper." Listen to these comments because this person they're talking about will be the one to please. Don't waste time showing the amiable Peaceful Phlegmatic houses that violate the mate's feelings, because they live in fear of upsetting the Powerful Choleric. Once the Peaceful Phlegmatic has found a few possibilities, expect the mate to blow in, race through them, and either reject them all as impossibilities or buy one on the spot.

With cars, the procedure is similar to houses. If there is no Powerful Choleric on the horizon, Peaceful Phlegmatics will shop, look, and think it over cautiously. They may come in one day to look around, and then, months later when you've forgotten them, they'll show up and want to test drive the same cars all over again. One Peaceful Phlegmatic man recounted that he spent almost a year testing different cars each Sunday afternoon. It was a pleasant way to relax, and he ultimately did buy a used car that was "good enough for me."

In presenting a network plan to Peaceful Phlegmatics, realize they will show almost no enthusiasm for what you are saying. You will have trouble reading their response. Popular Sanguines will get excited over the prospects of more money to spend, Powerful Cholerics will judge quickly whether the prospects are genuine, and Perfect Melancholies will ask detailed questions. Peaceful Phlegmatics will just sit there. They are tuned in to other people's feelings and will sway to whatever side seems to be winning. They will never buck the crowd, and they won't venture a strong opinion before they test the waters. They will never be aggressive salespeople, but they will be steady and win others by their low-key sincerity.

As you apply these examples into your business you will have a definite edge over competitors who don't know how to quickly assess the customer. Remember: Always sell not out of *your* personality but into *theirs*.

CHAPTER **19**

Practicing the Personality Puzzle

It's time for the final exam. You have learned how to spot the pieces of the Personality Puzzle in a crowd. You know where each piece fits in the whole picture. You understand how valuable every piece is to your workplace.

You have seen how an understanding of the Personality Puzzle can make a difference in business and in all relationships. Now let's look at some real-life personality problems and see how much fun it can be to put puzzles together.

Problem One: Compounding the Crisis

In the crisis care unit of a hospital three nurses formed a team. Nurse 1 was a Powerful Choleric, so efficient and on top of things that she had the job done before the orders were even written. She loved being in charge, thrived on crisis, and could run the whole place by herself. She looked at the other two as gap-fillers, under her control, even though each one had specific responsibilities.

Nurse 2 was a Popular Sanguine. The patients all loved her. She entertained them and lifted their spirits. Patients' families were appreciative of her willingness to talk with them, even though her information was not always accurate.

Nurse 3 was Peaceful Phlegmatic. She had a calming bedside manner, handled crises quietly, and was in awe of Nurse 1, who treated her like a slave.

One evening when the unit seemed at rest, Nurse 3 was asked to assist on a different floor where a crisis had arisen. Not daring to approach Nurse 1 for fear of conflict, she told Nurse 2 where she was going, why she was leaving, and the number where she could be reached if she were needed. In her Peaceful Phlegmatic mind she had covered all bases and avoided having to communicate with Nurse 1. Since there were no crises to handle, Nurse 2 wandered into the waiting room in search of an audience. She found a sad group in need of relief.

All is calm, all is bright. Powerful Choleric Nurse 1 is in charge, Popular Sanguine Nurse 2 is entertaining, and Peaceful Phlegmatic Nurse 3 is selflessly helping others.

Suddenly another crisis arose, and Nurse 1 got on the intercom with urgent requests for Nurse 2 and Nurse 3 to rush to her aid *right now!* Neither one responded. Nurse 2 was so involved in her story that she didn't hear the page, and Nurse 3 was on another floor. Nurse 1 was furious. Where were these women when she needed them? How dare they have left without telling her? The angrier she got the faster she ran, and she handled the crisis on her own. I'll show them.

Soon Nurse 3 sauntered back and asked calmly, "How are things going?" Nurse 1 turned in a rage and shouted, "Where have you been?" Nurse 3 stepped back in fear as Nurse 2 bounced in basking in the affirming response of the waiting room audience. As she saw the fury in Nurse 1 and the fear in Nurse 3, reality hit. "Oh darn! Did I forget to tell you that she had left the unit? Oops isn't that just like me?" She laughed at the situation expecting her humor to heal the hurts. You can imagine how funny Nurse 1 thought she was.

COMMENTARY

This situation really happened, perhaps in a hospital near you. If you were there, how would you have handled the situation differently? Play the whole scene over in your mind, putting into practice what you know about the Personality Puzzle.

All three participants made mistakes. Confrontation and anger could have been avoided if the three nurses had understood themselves and recognized how they each fit into the Personality Puzzle. Each one was an obvious clear personality. No one had to give them tests to determine their natures.

Nurse 1 needed to establish rapport with her team so they weren't scared to death of her. She had to treat them like equals not like slaves. If she had built respect and not fear Nurse 3 would have dared to report where she was going instead of leaving a message with Nurse 2.

Nurse 3 had worked with this team long enough to know that Nurse 2 was not a dependable message taker. She made a mistake in judgment by trusting her with the number of where she could be reached. She took the chance rather than risk a conflict with Nurse 1.

Popular Sanguine Nurse 2 meant well. She cheerfully gave Nurse 3 permission to leave and meant to cover for her if trouble arose. She had the best of intentions. But when she found a somber group in need of a laugh, she set her responsibilities adrift and floated off into fun. A Popular Sanguine's moving mouth shuts down her ears and Nurse 2 never heard the page. Can you see why Nurse 1 was furious, Nurse 3 frightened, and Nurse 2 amazed that anyone could be mad at her?

How could this scenario have been different? Powerful Choleric had to be approachable, Peaceful Phlegmatic had to dare to report to the right person, and Popular Sanguine had to take her responsiblities seriously. They didn't have to change their basic natures but they did need to see their areas of weakness and work to overcome them. A simple understanding of the Personality Puzzle could have saved the situation.

Problem Two: Heading into Strengths

Are the pieces fitting together in your mind? Is the Personality Puzzle starting to fall into place? Try another.

Betsy writes:

One shift I had a premature infant who had a patent ductus arteriosus (PDA), which is common in premature infants. (It is a small opening in the heart that should be open in utero, but closed at birth. When an infant is stressed the PDA may opene. One can usually hear a small murmur when auscultating the heart when the ductus is open after birth.) The murmur would come and go on this infant, and we were watching to see if the baby was going into failure due to the PDA's being open. That morning, I listened with the stethoscope to the infant's chest and heard a small murmur. When the resident came by, I mentioned that the murmur was present and that there were other clinical signs that could possibly indicate that the PDA was open. This was a fairly new resident who was a Powerful Choleric and was not about to let a nurse tell him anything. He listened to the chest but did not hear the murmur and stated, "You are wrong. There is no murmur. All you hear is the ventilator!" After he left, I listened again and the murmur was still there.

Betsy had discovered a problem that needed a solution, but she hit the Powerful Choleric resident wrong by telling him what she had discovered. His defenses went up, and his ears went deaf.

A while later, the cardiologist came by to check on the patient with the Powerful Choleric resident by his side. He asked how the infant was doing, and I stated that I had heard a murmur and described it, plus some other clinical symptoms. The cardiologist took out his stethoscope and listened. He turned to me and said, "You have good ears to pick up that murmur with your stethoscope. Let's go ahead and order a heart echo to rule out PDA." Being part Powerful Choleric myself I had to give the resident a "so-there" look.

Because the Powerful Choleric resident felt humiliated he was angry at Betsy. Even though the cardiologist didn't know of the previous episode, the resident was offended and sought retribution by insulting Betsy whenever possible. This minor event caused a friction that was never healed.

COMMENTARY

How could this situation have been prevented? If you were Betsy, what would you do?

Obviously, if we could deal with the resident we would show him that he may someday be wrong again, that his stubbornness could risk patients' lives, and that he must be open to other people's suggestions. He is not God, and he needs a teachable spirit if he is ever to fulfill his potential. What about Betsy? Could she have been more sensitive to the resident's desire to be right?

As she looks back on the situation with understanding, she realizes she shouldn't have told him what she had found but helped him to find it.

I could have been more successful in getting the resident to consider the possiblity of a murmur if I had put the stethoscope on the infant's chest where I had heard the murmur the loudest and asked his opinion of what he thought. He possibly would have been less defensive and more willing to listen to a nurse.

I have learned from experience that the various personalities must be taken into account in order to get desired results and increased efficiency.

Betsy has now learned how important it is to lead into the other person's strengths instead of pointing out weaknesses.

Problem Three: Declining Profits and Departing Employees

Let's look at Walt's problem. As the CEO of a manufacturing business, Walt took the company from the brink of bankruptcy to a comfortable profit situation. He did this in spite of Leo, the Popular Sanguine manager who had no concept of fiscal responsibility and who only wanted to take clients out to lunch and have fun. Unfortunately, because of his years with the company, manager Leo was paid a salary equal to Walt's. Because he didn't work much, Leo had enough spare time to keep Mr. Briggs, the president of the parent company, happy and impressed. While Powerful Choleric Walt was working, Leo was out getting the credit, speaking at banquets, and glad-handing potential clients with promises Walt couldn't keep.

In desperation, Walt went to Mr. Briggs, a pleasant academic Peaceful Phlegmatic who had maintained his position by avoiding conflict and causing no one any problems. Since he liked Leo's amusing personality and saw Walt as someone who was rocking the boat, Briggs listened and remained noncommittal. He referred Walt and his suggestions to Frank, a staff member who was supposed to be the liaison between the parent company and Walt's division. Amazingly enough, this Powerful Choleric man agreed with Walt that Leo was dead wood, getting too high a salary for doing little, and should be sent packing. Walt was given the authority to replace Leo with a person who would produce results at a lower salary. Since Walt had "inherited" Leo when he came to the company, he was thrilled that he could clean house and really get things under control. He was to make his plans and report back to Frank in a week. That weekend Frank went to an industry convention where he was offered a better job that he accepted immediately.

When Walt went for his appointment on Monday a blasé secretary told him, "Oh I guess I should have called you. Frank's got a new job and he's not coming back."

Walt couldn't believe it. He called Mr. Briggs and tried to get him to approve Frank's decision. Since Mr. Briggs was only three years from retirement and didn't want to make any waves, he would have no part of firing Leo and told Walt to wait until Frank's replacement came. Months went by. Leo continued to play. Walt kept doing the work and became increasingly frustrated. Finally Paul, a Peaceful Phlegmatic man, was chosen for Frank's job. Leo courted his attention immediately and when Walt went to explain his position and problems, Paul said he thought Leo was a "nice enough person," and he was intending to make no changes for at least a year.

In his frustration, Walt sent out resumes and got a job in a larger business quite quickly. No one tried to keep him or offered him any new perks, they just let him go. He couldn't believe none of these men seemed to care.

COMMENTARY

This whole situation was the proverbial comedy of errors. Mr. Briggs, the Peaceful Phlegmatic president of the parent company, did not want to make any decisions for fear he'd be held accountable if something went wrong. He liked, in his own terms, "to stay above it all." Frank saw the point, and agreed with Walt that Leo had to go. But he left no agenda behind when he suddenly took off. Paul, the new Peaceful Phlegmatic, didn't want to make any hasty decisions. Here was a sizable company full of irresponsible individuals. Mr. Briggs should have investigated the problem or at least had someone close to him check it out and report back to him. Frank shouldn't have walked off the job without some notice and transfer of authority. Paul didn't really need a whole year to think it over.

Because of the lack of concern, the company was left leaderless when Walt departed. Leo became CEO and was thrilled to have a bigger title. Within a year the volume of sales had dropped by half, and no one seemed to know why or care.

Understanding the Personality Puzzle we can see how the leaders were functioning in their weaknesses and not in their strengths. The Peaceful Phlegmatics, Mr. Briggs and Paul, were indecisive and avoided responsibility, the Powerful Choleric Frank was impulsive and thought only about his own future, and the Popular Sanguine Leo was playing and avoiding work. Adding these negatives together, the company lost Walt, the one key person who was willing to work and who was responsible for the salvation of the business from its past mistakes. Now the whole company is functioning in its weaknesses and is headed toward financial disaster.

What would you do if you were Mr. Briggs and in charge of trying to salvage a division that is performing poorly? How would you use your new found understanding of the personality puzzle to save this situation?

Case History One: Building a Business with the Personality Puzzle

According to the Health Care Financing Administration, spending on home health care grew more than any other segment of the health care industry in the 1980s. While nursing home care went up 10.3 percent, home health care grew 17.8 percent in annual spending.

Jackie, a Perfect Melancholy businesswoman, caught the trend early on and founded Preferred Home Health Care. The company, with eight area offices, is still growing. When Jackie and her Popular Sanguine sister Pam came to our Personality Plus seminar, their business was just beginning to explode, and they knew they needed help. They grabbed on to the practical application of the Personality Puzzle and began to use the material in their hiring policies and personnel training. When applicants come in, Pam gives them the Personality Profile explaining that the results won't be used to judge them or eliminate them but to place them where they will function in their strengths. They explain that we all have weaknesses, and we don't want to have a job where we are working every day in our areas of weakness. It is too exhausting and will result in failure.

The applicants are usually content to take the profile when they see it represents a caring attitude on the side of the potential employer and that there is no right or wrong.

Pam next asks applicants to describe their personality and looks to see if their opinion of themselves is consistent with the profile results. She watches their body language for shifting of feet or eyes indicating they may be trying to give the "right answers" instead of telling the truth. She also checks to see if their clothing fits what they say they are. One young woman maintained she was Perfect Melancholy while wearing a see-through chiffon mini-dress with tiger print fur boots on her tapping feet. Somehow it didn't all add up.

Next she gives them a hypothetical situation they might face, offers four possible good reactions, and asks which they would choose. This exercise validates the profile scores and the applicants' own opinion of themselves.

Next she calls for references from the last job. When the former employer won't give a verbal description, Pam offers them a composite of the probable personality strengths and weaknesses and asks if that fits the person in question. She says the reference person is often dumbfounded at the accuracy of her summary of the applicant, whom she has only just met.

In each of her offices, Jackie has placed the personalities where they will do the best possible work for the company. She has a Peaceful Phlegmatic director in each unit to keep peace with all the staff and to provide balance in a business that thrives on emergencies. She has Popular Sanguine receptionists, the first contact potential customers have. Since each person who comes into the office is nervous about bringing strangers into their home to care for their ailing loved ones, the first impression must be warm and gracious. The Popular Sanguine is never at a loss for words and makes everyone feel welcome.

Jackie has found that Peaceful Phlegmatics and Perfect Melancholies are the best at keeping the medical records in order and don't mind being away from the up-front action. They always know where to find the needed information. Perhaps the most crucial position is that of staffing coordinator, the one who has to handle the calls for help and charm the nurses into showing up when and where they are needed. Popular Sanguines are good at charm, but they give up too easily if the nurse doesn't want the assignment. Peaceful Phlegmatics are too easygoing and don't motivate the nurses to action. A combination Powerful Choleric/Perfect Melancholy seems to be ideal. They are clear and firm and won't give up until they have the situation handled correctly. Jackie has found that when she varies from this pattern she always regrets it. For salespeople Popular Sanguines/Powerful Cholerics are the best combination. They have outgoing personalities *and* can remember where they have been, a feat that's difficult for pure Popular Sanguines. The Super Powerful Cholerics don't like to take direction; they go where they want to go; and they tend to offend potential customers who don't see their point quickly.

In order to help the staffing coordinators in understanding their employees, Pam prints on the front of each "personnel packet" the name, personality, and emotional needs of each individual.

With little more than a glance at the front of the prepared personnel

---

Mary Smith

Popular Sanguine:
  Needs attention and approval for everything she does

Powerful Choleric:
  Wants you to notice how hard she works and wants
  you to express loyal support

Helen Johnson

Perfect Melancholy:
 Wants sentitivity and deep understanding

Peaceful Phlegmatic:
 Hopes you will value her a a person

---

packet, each coordinator can get a feel for the emotional needs of each nurse or staff member and know how to handle them.

Pam teaches the nurses how to recognize the personality of their homebound patients and then how to deal with them. This knowledge makes their work easier. Popular Sanguines are happy to see nurses arrive, as it means company, someone to talk to. They can be cheerful in illness if it brings them attention, presents, and flowers. They hope you will notice their new nightgown and how many cards they have received.

Powerful Cholerics tend to treat nurses like servants and boss them around. They hate any infirmity and become more impatient than ever if confined and unable to control their own bodies. They need nurses who are firm and encouraging. "You'll be up and out in no time."

Perfect Melancholies let nurses know whether they're on time or not and are sure the pill bottle won't get put back in the right place. They somewhat enjoy their ill health. It justifies their predictions that they would contract some malady. They often comment that no one ever comes to see them but nurses. Let them moan and groan, and tell them you understand.

Peaceful Phlegmatics don't seem to mind an occasional illness. They can rest easily and are grateful to have anyone paying attention to them. They are model patients and seem to thrive in physical adversity. They want you to be their friend and praise them for their patience.

Jackie runs the business and her Popular Sanguine sister Pam does the training, and consulting for those who will be interviewing. Many times a year Pam does a Personality Puzzle training workshop for the staff in each location. She teaches about the four personalities and reemphasizes that weaknesses are strengths carried too far. She finds they respond better to the idea that these flaws aren't really weaknesses but strengths out of balance. They all want to be functioning in their strengths. She uses examples that fit their business and keeps a sense of humor to help them enjoy the time of teaching. At the conclusion of the four-hour session she has all participants write down three areas where they need improvement and asks them to pray about the necessary changes. They then have lunch together where they discuss problems and are free to ask Pam questions. Both Pam and Jackie have found that their understanding and use of the four personalities has helped them to build a successful business in only a few years and to outrun their competition.

Case History Two: Cultivating the Landscape

Remember the story of Bonnie and her landscaping business in the Introduction? As we have worked with Bonnie for the last two years, her business has gone from shaky to profitable. She has taught her staff members to understand their personalities and to work in harmony with each other. Recently she asked each of them to write a summary of what they perceived to be their job description. Perfect Melancholy Roger typed his summary neatly, gave detailed descriptions, and met the deadline. Peaceful Phlegmatic Harry didn't want to bother writing it all out because he didn't think Bonnie would read it. Popular Sanguine Jim wanted to talk about it. Clara the one Powerful Choleric and the new supervisor of the team, called Bonnie the night before the report was due and stated clearly, "I have better things to do than to write out a job summary." Bonnie accepted her opinion and waited. Sure enough the next day when Clara saw others pass in their reports, she felt guilty and didn't want to come across as the one rebel in the group. She wrote a typically Powerful Choleric paper saying that she liked the flexibility of her job, the competent people she worked with, and the responsibility of sending crews out to do the landscaping. She then listed the things that disturbed her, in order of importance, and concluded with the fact that some of her problems come "because I'm trying to do too many things at one time." She added, "I feel uncomfortable trying to solve problems for which I have no easy solution."

Peaceful Phlegmatic all-purpose Laura, once she decided to do it, wrote such a beautiful description of her job and such an insightful understanding of the Personality Puzzle that we're including it to show the benefits of this knowledge in the workplace.

I consider myself to be both Popular Sanguine and Peaceful Phlegmatic. Deep inside I have found I am happier (more at peace) with my Popular Sanguine side. It's the Peaceful Phlegmatic traits in me that I do not like about myself. I am fortunate to have a varied job description. (I like variety!) Handling advertising has been part of my job description since I first started working here. It's not the most exciting work, but I realize its importance. It appeals to the Peaceful Phlegmatic side because a lot of it involves sitting around in the office. (I can even listen to my walkman.) It doesn't require a lot of original thought. I have to keep motivating myself to be sure the work gets done. (Run the show so to speak.) Also the Peaceful Phlegmatic needs to be motivated to get out and shoot photos. (Once I'm out the door, the Popular Sanguine can take over and make a fun time out of it.)

I primarily consider myself to be a landscape designer. This is the most meaningful part of my job. The Popular Sanguine in me loves this part. I get to go out and meet people, and get them excited about plants. Then I get to exercise my creative side and design, draw, and color a pretty plan. Naturally bidding the job doesn't appeal to the Popular Sanguine or the Peaceful Phlegmatic because it involves a lot of details and numbers. I have had to develop Perfect Melancholy systems to help keep me organized and accurate. There are drawbacks to being a Peaceful Phlegmatic salesperson, namely motivating the customer to buy.

Supervising the installation is probably the most "out of character" task I perform as part of my job. It involves giving instructions to others (Peaceful Phlegmatics aren't comfortable with this) and attention to details (not fun for the Popular Sanguine—it forces them to be organized).

Since I started working here, I have enjoyed watching the various plants bloom and change throughout the seasons. The Peaceful Phlegmatic finds peace in nature, while the Popular Sanguine responds to nature's beauty.

In using the Personality Puzzle in the workplace, Bonnie has, over the past year, had her salespeople write the personality of the customer on their work orders. This made it possible to go back through 1991 and come up with some fascinating statistics. She made up a chart for her own interest and found that Popular Sanguines were the easiest to sell to and bought the most.

Landscape Sales 1991

Customer Personalities	Percent of Jobs Sold	Percent of Gross Sales	Average Job
Sanguine	32	47	$5,773.13
Melancholy	39	32	$4,290.26
Choleric	3	3	$4,470.18
Phlegmatic	25	17	$2,936.54

Bonnie wrote:

Most of our sales went to Sanguines and Melancholies. Although we sold more Melancholies, the size of the job was considerably smaller than the average Sanguine job. Phlegmatics were easy to sell although they spent the least of all. Cholerics think they know more about land-scaping than we do—so normally they want to do it themselves or feel that we're not sensitive to their desires and so we don't sell them. As we reviewed the complaints for the year we found that every problem customer we had was a Melancholy.

Can you see the benefits of what Bonnie has done? She has not only taught the Personality Puzzle to her staff, but has had them add the customer's personality to the work order. This benefits the business and shows the staff the practicality of using the personalities in sales situations.

When the Pieces Don't Fit

Using the Personality Profile gives us a tool to help in understanding and accepting others as they are. We can see the value of having everyone function in their strengths and not in their weaknesses. But is everybody normal?

Let's assume that we all started out normal, that we were born with a direction of personality and with responses that grew out of our own natures. We also have emotional needs that vary with our innate personalities. It is generally accepted that our greatest human urge is self-preservation and our greatest need is love. We all try to save ourselves from harm, and we respond to someone who loves us. Added to these basics are our emotional needs according to our own personalities. The Popular Sanguine not only is self-protective and looking for love but craves an abundance of attention, approval, affection, and acceptance. When these needs are not met at home the Popular Sanguine child hangs on to mother, becomes bad to get attention, talks constantly, and/or hits others for some sort of response. As teens they become the center of attention, loudest in the group. They will do whatever it takes, illegal or immoral, to be accepted by their peers.

By the time you meet troubled Popular Sanguines in business they may be extremely loud, desperate for attention, exaggerating to the point of lying, easily led into temptation, openly sexual in word and action. They may treat everyone to lunch and give lavish presents beyond their means in hopes of receiving love and approval in return. They aim to become the boss's pet in an attempt to gain the "parental" approval they didn't receive as children. They will become the doting slave of anyone who will mother them, tell them constantly that they are adorable and precious, and laugh warmly at their humor. If you praise them in front of others and build them up whenever possible they will be eternally grateful. You are giving them what they have always needed.

Perfect Melancholy children thrive in a quiet, orderly home when at least one parent is a sensitive Perfect Melancholy and understands their deep artistic nature. But put these children in a group of loud, aggressive, fast-paced achievers and they will wither away in a corner. Perfect Melancholies' fear of social occasions and desire for quiet means they may become loners in a family that doesn't understand them. They may stay away from group activities and respond only to a teacher who sees their depth and talent and reaches in to pull it out. They may show little enthusiasm for family fun and appear to the rest to be always depressed. If their families perceive them as wet blankets, they may be ignored and left out of activities.

By the time you meet troubled Perfect Melancholies in business they may feel that nobody understands them. If you take the time to talk with them, quietly with the door shut, and ask for their feelings on any subject, they will gladly give them and consider you a person of depth, caring, and sensitivity. Perfect Melancholies will think things over before making a move and will do accurate work. Just give them a quiet place to work away from the chatty Popular Sanguines and the bossy Powerful Cholerics. Let them know you believe in them, and don't get depressed yourself when they have a down day.

Powerful Cholerics, who have the strongest sense of survival, need love in the form of affirmation for achievement. They want to know that the family is with them, not against them. They look at life as a potential battleground. They constantly size up which side others are on. All is black or white with Powerful Cholerics. As children they wanted to be in charge of things and be praised for all they did. If these needs were not met at home, they became overly controlling at school, bossing around everyone, including the teacher, and becoming the playground bullies. As Powerful Cholerics reach teenage years they usually become leaders, good or bad —the class president or the rebel—according to how their emotional needs have been met and considering which of the groups look up to them for direction. A teacher said of Marita, "I hope she decides to head in the right direction, because if she doesn't she'll lead everyone right over the cliff of destruction."

By the time you meet Powerful Cholerics who have emotional problems they have learned to cover them with confidence and bravado, making most people see them as super achievers. They will work hard in search of affirmation, seek control that isn't even in their department, and manipulate behind your back. They will do more work than any other personality, but don't take a long vacation and leave them in charge.

Peaceful Phlegmatic children are by far the easiest ones to raise because they are born wanting to please others and avoid all conflict. They will agree with their parents' opinions and try to mediate between warring family members. They will eat whenever and whatever they are fed uncomplainingly. These passive children stay out of trouble, but by the time they are teenagers and feel they aren't as aggressive and magnetic as their friends, they tend to be easily led astray by adventurous heroes. As teens they begin to upset Powerful Choleric parents because they don't seem to have any motivation. The parents want to know when they're going to get off the couch and get moving. The more the parents push, the more the Peaceful Phlegmatic children resist.

By the time you meet troubled Peaceful Phlegmatics in business they may be insecure in their performance and not feel they're worth much. They are looking for someone to tell them that they're of great value even though they're not super-achievers. Their worth in the business is often from what they *don't* do: agitate, interfere, start trouble, talk too much, or appear moody. They provide balance and tone down the hysteria of other personalities. They may have a dry sense of humor that can turn sarcastic and could be hurtful. But it's just their low-key way of venting long-suppressed feelings.

As business people, we would like to feel that not many of the people we work with have emotional problems. But in the surveys we have cited in Fred's book, *Promise of Restoration* (Thomas Nelson, 1990, p. 100), 75 percent of the women and 60 percent of the men were victimized in some way as children. In a university preparing students to be psychologists and counselors, only 3 graduates out of 96 did not need psychological help themselves. Although we are not called to be psychiatrists, having some general information on possible personality problems can save all of us time and trouble.

No one sets out to be a problem. No little child says "I think I'll try to become obnoxious." If you are faced with emotionally unstable people in your business today, you can assume they have suffered some kind of trauma in childhood.

Popular Sanguines felt neglected, lost in the shuffle. No one responded to their humor and personality. They are still desperate for attention from anyone who will give it. In business, Popular Sanguine victims become compulsive talkers often stretching the truth. They are desperate for attention and will go to extremes to get it.

Powerful Cholerics were held under control, and no matter how much they achieved, it wasn't enough. They are still trying to show father that they are successful. In the workplace, Powerful Choleric victims become compulsive workers, controlling everyone, desperate for success. They will push themselves to achieve it.

Perfect Melancholies felt their parents were insensitive to their needs. They became easily hurt and put down. They "analyzed" that everyone else got more time, love, and support than they did. They are still feeling rejected and are seeking someone who will truly understand them. Perfect Melancholy victims become the nit-picking perfectionists desperate for understanding and sensitivity and will easily sink into depression when things aren't in order.

Peaceful Phlegmatics were overlooked and ignored because they were quiet and undemanding. They were made fun of because they weren't bubbly like the Popular Sanguine sister, aggressive like the Powerful Choleric brother, or intellectual like the Perfect Melancholy cousin. They still feel insecure and wish someone would value them for who they are and not just what they accomplish. Peaceful Phlegmatic victims don't exhibit compulsions, but as adult victims of childhood trauma, they feel worthless, tend to be self-deprecating, and sometimes shut down all feelings.

Before making negative judgments on some of the people who seem to fail repeatedly, realize that they may have been hurt or rejected as children.

When we understand the normal personality behaviors, we can more easily spot those with emotional problems. It is important for us all to realize that childhood trauma often produces adult compulsions. Although we can't become psychologists we can learn to spot aberrant behavior and not waste our time trying to solve the wrong problems.

If you find people who fit in any of these categories of emotional pain, we recommend that you read our book *Freeing Your Mind from Memories That Bind*. Have copies on hand to give to those in need. This book takes each personality and analyzes its background, helping people to see where their difficulties have come from. The list of adult symptoms of childhood abuse in the back of the book will be a helpful indicator of potential problems and save you from putting perpetual Band-Aids over past but recurring patterns.

CHAPTER 20

Fitting the Personality Puzzle Together in Your Workplace

We've reviewed the *visible, various,* and *valuable* pieces of the Personality Puzzle. Knowing who's who among your employees or coworkers is the first step. Knowing their differences and how they're likely to react in different situations is the second. Knowing their value to an organization, their strengths and weaknesses and needs is the third. Putting it all together is a process that begins with you, no matter what place in any of the organizations you find yourself in.

Although this checklist is written primarily for those in some kind of management or leadership position, it will equally apply to those of you who may not at the moment be in charge. We all are dealing with people in relationships that are not perfect so as you go over the checklist apply it to fit your particular needs.

1. Examine your own personality and work style.

Before using this information to spot the personalities of those you work with, take the time to evaluate your own personality. It is difficult to inspire others to introspection unless you can show what you have learned and how you have applied your knowledge. When your staff sees a kinder, gentler boss and observes that you can occasionally laugh at your own mistakes, they will want to know why.

As you evaluate yourself, have family members, down-line workers, or coworkers do the Personality Profile for you. Then calmly discuss their opinions. Don't defend yourself. Accept what they say and thank them for their candid appraisal. If you refute or argue they will cease their suggestions and go back to the phony relationship they may have had with you before. Encourage their honesty, thank them for it, and let them see your desire to change.

2. Check your own compulsions.

The word *compulsion* means "pulled into something," drawn toward negative behavior, magnetized by pornography, gambling, alcohol, or drugs. On a lesser scale Popular Sanguines often become compulsive shoppers, spending money they don't have. Powerful Cholerics can become compulsive workers and controllers needing to be in charge of everyone. Perfect Melancholies may become compulsive loners retreating into ivory towers where all is perfect. Peaceful Phlegmatics may become so indecisive that they can't get out of bed and move into the mainstream of life. Ask yourself, "Is there anything in my life that is usurping my energy, that is controlling me, that I can't resist?" Ask others if they see any of your behavior patterns that are carried to extremes.

How important it is for each of us to recognize our compulsions and pull back before we have gone too far.

3. Lighten up!

Don't take yourself so seriously that people don't dare to be themselves when they are near you. For Popular Sanguines lightening up is no problem, but for Powerful Cholerics who want the work done now and Perfect Melancholies who insist life be perfect, there may be a need to allow a few minutes a day for fun. Fun, you say? Fun at work?

A new study by Kurt Kraiger at the University of Colorado reports that "fun breaks" in the middle of a pressured day will increase productivity and give the workers fresh enthusiasm for the task at hand. Professor Kraiger provided a comedy video for 80 people to watch and found that after viewing, their interest level and stimulation was far higher than those who had not watched. The "fun break" had lifted their moods and made them more excited about their work.

Popular Sanguines no doubt loved this experiment. And Peaceful Phlegmatics found it restful. Since Professor Kraiger didn't take the personalities into account, we won't know whether the Powerful Cholerics found this time wasteful and the Perfect Melancholies thought it was trivial. But the idea may be a fresh thought for some of you "nose to the grindstone" types.

The conclusion to this experiment is that you may get more out of your employees if you encourage them to take guilt-free "fun breaks" such as walks or other exercise, occasional long lunches, or just time to rest. Remember: A spoonful of sugared humor helps the medicine go down.

4. Treat coworkers and employees as real people with feelings.

On 17 February 1992, *Newsweek* published the results of a survey aimed at finding out what motivates people to work hard and to succeed. The prime motivator, with an 89 percent positive response rate, was "Self-esteem/the way people feel about themselves." Far below was fear of failure at 44 percent and status in the eyes of others at 35 percent.

Stop and think about how you treat others. Does what you say do them a favor and lift their self-esteem? If it does and you are making others feel good about themselves, they will want to work hard for you.

Conversely, if your comments, gestures, and facial expressions and commands are so authoritative and demeaning that you put down the other person, you wipe out their natural motivation and force them into working out of fear.

Read our book *Silver Boxes: The Gift of Encouragement* to understand the value of positive words. (See Appendix D for full publishing information.)

5. Be a reliable leader.

So often bosses feel they can do whatever they want because they are in charge. But to produce a team effort the leader has to be reliable. People have to know they can count on you to do what you say you will do. If you call a meeting, do you remember to show up on time? If you say you'll review salaries on June 1, do you remember to do it? If you promise a new copying machine, do you go out and buy it? Don't use your personality weaknesses as an excuse for your lax behavior. No matter what your personality, you need to build trust with your people. They need to know that if you say something, they can count on your follow-through.

6. Analyze the personalities of your team.

Now that you have yourself in order, it is time to look at others. Make a list of all the jobs under your jurisdiction, write a brief description of each job, and add a note of which personality type would function best in this responsibility. Now observe who actually holds these positions. In how many cases do you have the right person in the right place? If you are at 100 percent, you either have fantastic analytical ability or you are very lucky. If you see that you have people struggling in their areas of weakness, begin to sort this out and shift responsibilities until the whole puzzle fits together.

7. Staff your weaknesses.

As you look over the people you have and analyze your own abilities, you may find some gaping holes in your workplace. Determine what personalities you are missing, and then look to staff your weaknesses or the weaknesses of the business as a whole. Go back in this book to the part about advertising for specific personalities. Read it over again, and begin a search for the right person. Experience and ability are always important, but try to find the individual whose personality will fill in your weaknesses.

8. Teach your team about the personalities.

You will increase your understanding of the personalities you work with by becoming knowledgeable even if you never share this concept with your staff. But if you do teach the others you will increase productivity and office morale. Suddenly lights will go on in their minds as they find explanations for their own desires and the behavior of others.

You can do what Jackie and Pam have done in the home health care business in whatever field you are in. They feel that the time they have spent in giving personality workshops has been more than worth the effort. They have not only put people in the right places, but they have shown them why. Morale is high and the business is outstripping the competition in their area.

Bonnie has taught her landscaping staff how to use the personalities in selling and has recorded the results enabling them all to concentrate on the Popular Sanguines and Perfect Melancholies for the coming year. It's not that they will only sell to these two, but they have the statistics to show that the Powerful Cholerics do their own work and the Peaceful Phlegmatics take a long time to make decisions and tend to buy less. Whatever your business is, teach your people to understand themselves and others.

9. Treat everyone fairly.

Often I get the comment that the boss obviously loves or hates a certain type of personality. When this becomes public knowledge, people try to change to fit what they think you want and many end up wearing masks and being phonies. Nicholas wrote us after a seminar:

> As a metallurgical engineer I have worked for many types of employers. One company had a Powerful Choleric owner whose management style of absolute power prevailed throughout all the organization. His idea was "you agree with me or you're out!" Because of that I had six bosses in three and a half years. Some quit and others were fired. This was very stressful as each boss tried to change our personalities. In another oil company, the Powerful Choleric managers let us know that if we weren't strong and aggressive we would not move up the corporate ladder. If you were not bossy and demanding, you were not management material, so we all had to put on masks and try to be what they wanted. In the last company I worked for, a Fortune 500 company, the general of my division was a Powerful Choleric so Cholerics were more special to him, and we had to change our personalities to be more acceptable to him. Having to play all the different personality roles is too stressful and affects productivity. It would be so much better if they allowed us to perform with our own personalities and accept us for who we are instead of casting a new show with each new manager.

What a shame it is that so many managers with all kinds of education don't seem to know how to evaluate their people and encourage them to function in their strengths. If you can accept your staff as they are and not make them play an unfamiliar role, you will increase the energy and productivity of your team.

Playing an unnatural role is exhausting. Treat everyone fairly and remember that being different doesn't make a person wrong.

10. Provide materials, workshops, books, and tapes for your staff or network.

Always be on the alert for materials and programs that will help your team members feel good about themselves, provide further education, and lift group morale. After you've read this book, pass it around to others, or give each one a personal copy. If you don't feel able to teach your staff about the personalities or if you don't have time, ask a Popular Sanguine to do it for you. Popular Sanguines love to present programs and will usually study up if they are going to be in front of the group and get credit.

If you wish to have a speaker come in to share the Personality Puzzle give our office a call. Or if you wish to find personality books on different areas, please see the end of this book for a list of materials and information about how to contact CLASS.

Network Marketing

One of the reasons that network marketing is growing rapidly is that it provides motivational and inspirational books and tapes for those involved. From our own perspective as speakers at many networking conventions, we have concluded that whether or not the individuals make much money, they will become better people for the learning experience. They associate with people who are positive, who have a love of family, God, and country, and who help them feel better about themselves. These are all traits that will improve any business.

Business Review Weekly (24 Jan. 1992) did a cover story entitled "The Amway Army: Why Direct Selling Is Booming." The Australian magazine pointed out successes in its country and gave much of the credit to the workshops, books, and tapes that are used to improve personal life-styles as well as sell products.

> Most Amway distributors are husband-and-wife teams. Gail and Russell Jaoka joined the company in 1981. At the time, both worked as teachers and had part-time jobs to supplement their income. They are now "diamond" distributors running a network that turns over $5 million a year. Amway distributors are encouraged to work as a team. Some company rallies feature marriage relationship guidance sessions that stress the importance of the family unit.

In times of recession, it is both wise and practical to learn from the networkers and provide positive materials for the personal growth of our people.

Reinventing Ourselves

In choosing Ted Turner as Man of the Year for 1991, *Time* titled him "Prince of the Global Village" and commended him for having the vision to bring the world together through telecommunications and to present the dynamic events of war and peace to viewers in over 150 countries.

At the beginning of the cover story (6 Jan. 1992), *Time* gave a thought-provoking definition that should be pondered by all personalities who wish to become successful.

> Visionaries are possessed creatures, men and women in the thrall of belief so powerful that they ignore all else—even reason—to ensure that reality catches up with their dreams. . . . Always behind the action is an idea, a passionate sense of what is eternal in human nature and also of what is coming but as yet unseen, just over the horizon.

Was Ted Turner born to be a visionary? Was life always easy?

According to *Time* and many other articles, Ted was brought up by a father that was a stern disciplinarian, who set impossible expectations, and who never gave encouraging words. He felt that insecurity breeds greatness. He sent Ted to military school, criticized his choice of subjects, and made him pay rent during summer vacations. All of this caused obviously Powerful Choleric Ted to become a compulsive workaholic, to suppress his anger toward his father, and let it spill out on others. Ted was desperate for his father's approval of his abilities and achievements, but he never received the praise he craved. When his father committed suicide, Ted was left empty and alone. "Because I had counted on him to make the judgment of whether or not I was a success."

Ted exhibited the strengths of the Powerful Choleric personality, but they were carried to such an extreme that people were terrified of him. He put down his first wife in public, snapped at any slight imperfection in his children, and struck new members on his ship who made even trivial mistakes. He ran his business in military fashion and had bursts of verbal violence when things weren't done his way. Through all of this Ted was successful in the eyes of the world, but he ultimately came to realize that he was miserable within himself. Here is the perfect example of the Choleric who didn't get his emotional needs met as a child, who is still seeking powerful approval as an adult, who has become a compulsive workaholic, and who has emotional problems in the area of relationships.

Once Ted saw what he had done with himself, he decided to reinvent himself. He asked for opinions about his behavior and listened to those who dared tell him. He began some serious counseling and said of himself, "I started to listen and not be judgmental, and wait until someone was through rather than interrupting them, and then think about what they said before I prepared an answer. I learned to give and take better than I had previously."

Ted has purposely leveled out his roller-coaster emotional life and has determined to deal with his own personality weaknesses.

As we have found in our work with thousands of people, we tend to marry people on the same level of emotional pain. Ted has found Jane Fonda who comes prepacked with her own parallel problems: a mother who committed suicide, a father who was a harsh taskmaster, a period of rebellion, failed marriages, and problem children. She claims that she is repairing her dream and states, "By necessity, both of us created ourselves and then recreated ourselves a number of times."

No one can predict how this marriage will turn out, but at least they both are facing the reality of childhood trauma and working to overcome the results of their pain.

Priscilla Painton, author of the *Time* article on Turner, wrote, "I discovered that there was something new to say about him. He is a changed man not just because he fell madly in love or because he got older, but because he made an emotionally strenuous effort to grow up."

How About You?

In the beginning of this book we mentioned how many of us are walking through life with an empty toolbox. We want to build positive relationships, but we don't have the equipment we need to do so. We have tried to present tools that can be used to change lives, knowing that when we can hammer down our own personality we can begin to understand ourselves and build up others.

We've seen that there are *visible* differences that help us estimate probable personalities.

We've learned that there are *various* strengths and weaknesses in each individual and that we should examine ourselves to find out how we are doing.

We've discovered that all of us are *valuable* parts of the big picture and just because some of us are different we aren't wrong.

Our aim is not to jump into a contrasting personality but to work prayerfully and humanly to overcome our weaknesses and eliminate those traits that are offensive to others.

We don't need to reinvent ourselves but to follow the message of that old song that urges us to accentuate the positives, eliminate the negatives and not to mess with Mr. Inbetween.

If you are a Popular Sanguine, be grateful that you have a sense of humor and can tell stories that entertain the entire office, but develop a sensitivity as to when is the right time for fun. Cut out about half of what comes to your mind to say and try to stay closer to the truth.

If you are a Perfect Melancholy, cheer up and realize that every group needs a person who is sensitive, thoughtful, and accurate, but don't expect others to become perfectionists and then get depressed when they don't improve.

If you are a Powerful Choleric, you already know you are a born leader and can take control of every situation, but be sure you aren't so bossy that no one wants to respond to your instructions.

If you are a Peaceful Phlegmatic, realize that we all love your quiet, inoffensive, and gentle spirit, but don't become so passive that you can't make necessary decisions or offer opinions. We can't afford to sit around and wait for all those other people to improve. We have to take the first step.

So let's make that effort. Let's put all of the various pieces together in our Personality Puzzle so that we can create the beautiful picture we want our workplace to be.

APPENDICES

- ☐ *Your Personality Profile*
- ☐ *Personality Test Word Definitions*
- ☐ *Personality Summaries*
- ☐ *Valuable Resources*

Your Personality Profile

Directions—In *each* of the following rows of *four words across*, place an X in front of the *one* word that most often applies to you. Continue through all forty lines; be sure each number is marked. If you are not sure which word "most applies," ask a spouse or a friend, and think of what your answer would have been *when you were a child*. (Full definitions for each of these words begin on page 191.)

Strengths

1	___ Adventurous	___ Adaptable	___ Animated	___ Analytical
2	___ Persistent	___ Playful	___ Persuasive	___ Peaceful
3	___ Submissive	___ Self-sacrificing	___ Sociable	___ Strong-willed
4	___ Considerate	___ Controlled	___ Competitive	___ Convincing
5	___ Refreshing	___ Respectful	___ Reserved	___ Resourceful
6	___ Satisfied	___ Sensitive	___ Self-reliant	___ Spirited
7	___ Planner	___ Patient	___ Positive	___ Promoter
8	___ Sure	___ Spontaneous	___ Scheduled	___ Shy
9	___ Orderly	___ Obliging	___ Outspoken	___ Optimistic
10	___ Friendly	___ Faithful	___ Funny	___ Forceful
11	___ Daring	___ Delightful	___ Diplomatic	___ Detailed
12	___ Cheerful	___ Consistent	___ Cultured	___ Confident
13	___ Idealistic	___ Independent	___ Inoffensive	___ Inspiring
14	___ Demonstrative	___ Decisive	___ Dry humor	___ Deep
15	___ Mediator	___ Musical	___ Mover	___ Mixes easily
16	___ Thoughtful	___ Tenacious	___ Talker	___ Tolerant
17	___ Listener	___ Loyal	___ Leader	___ Lively
18	___ Contented	___ Chief	___ Chartmaker	___ Cute
19	___ Perfectionist	___ Pleasant	___ Productive	___ Popular
20	___ Bouncy	___ Bold	___ Behaved	___ Balanced

Weaknesses

21	___ Blank	___ Bashful	___ Brassy	___ Bossy
22	___ Undisciplined	___ Unsympathetic	___ Unenthusiastic	___ Unforgiving
23	___ Reticent	___ Resentful	___ Resistant	___ Repetitious
24	___ Fussy	___ Fearful	___ Forgetful	___ Frank
25	___ Impatient	___ Insecure	___ Indecisive	___ Interrupts
26	___ Unpopular	___ Uninvolved	___ Unpredictable	___ Unaffectionate
27	___ Headstrong	___ Haphazard	___ Hard to please	___ Hesitant
28	___ Plain	___ Pessimistic	___ Proud	___ Permissive
29	___ Angered easily	___ Aimless	___ Argumentative	___ Alienated
30	___ Naive	___ Negative attitude	___ Nervy	___ Nonchalant
31	___ Worrier	___ Withdrawn	___ Workaholic	___ Wants credit
32	___ Too sensitive	___ Tactless	___ Timid	___ Talkative
33	___ Doubtful	___ Disorganized	___ Domineering	___ Depressed
34	___ Inconsistent	___ Introvert	___ Intolerant	___ Indifferent
35	___ Messy	___ Moody	___ Mumbles	___ Manipulative
36	___ Slow	___ Stubborn	___ Show-off	___ Skeptical
37	___ Loner	___ Lord over others	___ Lazy	___ Loud
38	___ Sluggish	___ Suspicious	___ Short-tempered	___ Scatterbrained
39	___ Revengeful	___ Restless	___ Reluctant	___ Rash
40	___ Compromising	___ Critical	___ Crafty	___ Changeable

Personality Scoring Sheet

Now transfer all your X's to the corresponding words on the Personality Scoring Sheet, and add up your totals. For example, if you checked Animated on the profile, check it on the scoring sheet. (Note: The words are in a different order on the profile and the scoring sheet.)

Strengths

	Popular Sanguine	Powerful Choleric	Perfect Melancholy	Peaceful Phlegmatic
1	___ Animated	___ Adventurous	___ Analytical	___ Adaptable
2	___ Playful	___ Persuasive	___ Persistent	___ Peaceful
3	___ Sociable	___ Strong-willed	___ Self-sacrificing	___ Submissive
4	___ Convincing	___ Competitive	___ Considerate	___ Controlled
5	___ Refreshing	___ Resourceful	___ Respectful	___ Reserved
6	___ Spirited	___ Self-reliant	___ Sensitive	___ Satisfied
7	___ Promoter	___ Positive	___ Planner	___ Patient
8	___ Spontaneous	___ Sure	___ Scheduled	___ Shy
9	___ Optimistic	___ Outspoken	___ Orderly	___ Obliging
10	___ Funny	___ Forceful	___ Faithful	___ Friendly
11	___ Delightful	___ Daring	___ Detailed	___ Diplomatic
12	___ Cheerful	___ Confident	___ Cultured	___ Consistent
13	___ Inspiring	___ Independent	___ Idealistic	___ Inoffensive
14	___ Demonstrative	___ Decisive	___ Deep	___ Dry humor
15	___ Mixes easily	___ Mover	___ Musical	___ Mediator
16	___ Talker	___ Tenacious	___ Thoughtful	___ Tolerant
17	___ Lively	___ Leader	___ Loyal	___ Listener
18	___ Cute	___ Chief	___ Chartmaker	___ Contented
19	___ Popular	___ Productive	___ Perfectionist	___ Pleasant
20	___ Bouncy	___ Bold	___ Behaved	___ Balanced

Totals—Strengths

_____   _____   _____   _____

Weaknesses

	Popular Sanguine	Powerful Choleric	Perfect Melancholy	Peaceful Phlegmatic
21	___ Brassy	___ Bossy	___ Bashful	___ Blank
22	___ Undisciplined	___ Unsympathetic	___ Unforgiving	___ Unenthusiastic
23	___ Repetitious	___ Resistant	___ Resentful	___ Reticent
24	___ Forgetful	___ Frank	___ Fussy	___ Fearful
25	___ Interrupts	___ Impatient	___ Insecure	___ Indecisive
26	___ Unpredictable	___ Unaffectionate	___ Unpopular	___ Uninvolved
27	___ Haphazard	___ Headstrong	___ Hard to please	___ Hesitant
28	___ Permissive	___ Proud	___ Pessimistic	___ Plain
29	___ Angered easily	___ Argumentative	___ Alienated	___ Aimless
30	___ Naive	___ Nervy	___ Negative attitude	___ Nonchalant
31	___ Wants credit	___ Workaholic	___ Withdrawn	___ Worrier
32	___ Talkative	___ Tactless	___ Too sensitive	___ Timid
33	___ Disorganized	___ Domineering	___ Depressed	___ Doubtful
34	___ Inconsistent	___ Intolerant	___ Introvert	___ Indifferent
35	___ Messy	___ Manipulative	___ Moody	___ Mumbles
36	___ Show-off	___ Stubborn	___ Skeptical	___ Slow
37	___ Loud	___ Lord over others	___ Loner	___ Lazy
38	___ Scatterbrained	___ Short-tempered	___ Suspicious	___ Sluggish
39	___ Restless	___ Rash	___ Revengeful	___ Reluctant
40	___ Changeable	___ Crafty	___ Critical	___ Compromising

Totals—Weaknesses

____   ____   ____   ____

Combined Totals

____   ____   ____   ____

This test is very easy to interpret. Once you've transferred your answers to the scoring sheet, added up your total number of answers in each of the four columns, and added your totals from both the strengths and weaknesses sections, you'll know your dominant personality type. You'll also know what combination you are. If, for example, your score is 15 in Powerful Choleric strengths and weaknesses, there's really little question. You're almost all Powerful Choleric. But if your score is, for example, 8 in Popular Sanguine, 6 in Perfect Melancholy, and 2 in each of the others, you're a Powerful Choleric with a strong Perfect Melancholy. You'll also, of course, know your least dominant type.

As you read and work with the material in this book, you'll learn how to put your strengths to work for you, how to compensate for the weaknesses in your dominant type, and how to understand the strengths and weaknesses of other types.

Personality Test Word Definitions

Adapted by Fred Littauer from *Personality Patterns* by Lana Bateman.

STRENGTHS

1

Adventurous. One who will take on new and daring enterprises with a determination to master them.

Adaptable. Easily fits and is comfortable in any situation.

Animated. Full of life, lively use of hand, arm, and face gestures.

Analytical. Likes to examine the parts for their logical and proper relationships.

2

Persistent. Sees one project through to its completion before starting another.

Playful. Full of fun and good humor.

Persuasive. Convinces through logic and fact rather than charm or power.

Peaceful. Seems undisturbed and tranquil and retreats from any form of strife.

3

Submissive. Easily accepts any other's point of view or desire with little need to assert his own opinion.

Self-sacrificing. Willingly gives up his own personal being for the sake of, or to meet the needs of others.

Sociable. One who sees being with others as an opportunity to be cute and entertaining rather than as a challenge or business opportunity.

Strong-willed. Determined to have one's own way.

4

Considerate. Having regard for the needs and feelings of others.

Controlled. Has emotional feelings but rarely displays them.

Competitive. Turns every situation, happening, or game into a contest and always plays to win!

Convincing. Can win you over to anything through the sheer charm of his personality.

5

Refreshing. Renews and stimulates or makes others feel good.
Respectful. Treats others with deference, honor, and esteem.
Reserved. Self-restrained in expression of emotion or enthusiasm.
Resourceful. Able to act quickly and effectively in virtually all situations.

6

Satisfied. A person who easily accepts any circumstance or situation.
Sensitive. Intensively cares about others, and what happens.
Self-reliant. An independent person who can fully rely on his own capabilities, judgment, and resources.
Spirited. Full of life and excitement.

7

Planner. Prefers to work out a detailed arrangement beforehand, for the accomplishment of project or goal, and prefers involvement with the planning stages and the finished product rather than the carrying out of the task.
Patient. Unmoved by delay, remains calm and tolerant.
Positive. Knows it will turn out right if he's in charge.
Promoter. Urges or compels others to go along, join, or invest through the charm of his own personality.

8

Sure. Confident, rarely hesitates or wavers.
Spontaneous. Prefers all of life to be impulsive, unpremeditated activity, not restricted by plans.
Scheduled. Makes, and lives, according to a daily plan, dislikes his plan to be interrupted.
Shy. Quiet, doesn't easily instigate a conversation.

9

Orderly. Having a methodical, systematic arrangement of things.
Obliging. Accommodating. One who is quick to do it another's way.
Outspoken. Speaks frankly and without reserve.
Optimistic. Sunny disposition who convinces self and others that everything will turn out all right.

10

Friendly. A responder rather than an initiator, seldom starts a conversation.

Faithful. Consistently reliable, steadfast, loyal, and devoted sometimes beyond reason.

Funny. Sparkling sense of humor that can make virtually any story into an hilarious event.

Forceful. A commanding personality whom others would hesitate to take a stand against.

11

Daring. Willing to take risks; fearless, bold.

Delightful. A person who is upbeat and fun to be with.

Diplomatic. Deals with people tactfully, sensitively, and patiently.

Detailed. Does everything in proper order with a clear memory of all the things that happen.

12

Cheerful. Consistently in good spirits and promoting hapiness in others.

Consistent. Stays emotionally on an even keel, responding as one might expect.

Cultured. One whose interests involve both intellectual and artistic pursuits, such as theatre, symphony, ballet.

Confident. Self-assured and certain of own ability and success.

13

Idealistic. Visualizes things in their perfect form, and has a need to measure up to that standard himself.

Independent. Self-sufficient, self-supporting, self-confident and seems to have little need of help.

Inoffensive. A person who never says or causes anything unpleasant or objectionable.

Inspiring. Encourages others to work, join, or be involved, and makes the whole thing fun.

14

Demonstrative. Openly expresses emotion, especially affection, and doesn't hesitate to touch others while speaking to them.

Decisive. A person with quick, conclusive, judgment-making ability.

Dry humor. Exhibits "dry wit," usually one-liners which can be sarcastic in nature.

Deep. Intense and often introspective with a distaste for surface conversation and pursuits.

15

Mediator. Consistently finds him- or herself in the role of reconciling differences in order to avoid conflict.

Musical. Participates in or has a deep appreciation for music, is committed to music as an art form, rather than the fun of performance.

Mover. Driven by a need to be productive, is a leader whom others follow, finds it difficult to sit still.

Mixes easily. Loves a party and can't wait to meet everyone in the room, never meets a stranger.

16

Thoughtful. A considerate person who remembers special occasions and is quick to make a kind gesture.

Tenacious. Holds on firmly, stubbornly, and won't let go until the goal is accomplished.

Talker. Constantly talking, generally telling funny stories and entertaining everyone around, feeling the need to fill the silence in order to make others comfortable.

Tolerant. Easily accepts the thoughts and ways of others without the need to disagree with or change them.

17

Listener. Always seems willing to hear what you have to say.

Loyal. Faithful to a person, ideal, or job, sometimes beyond reason.

Leader. A natural born director, who is driven to be in charge, and often finds it difficult to believe that anyone else can do the job as well.

Lively. Full of life, vigorous, energetic.

18

Contented. Easily satisfied with what he has, rarely envious.

Chief. Commands leadership and expects people to follow.

Chartmaker. Organizes life, tasks, and problem solving by making lists, forms or graphs.

Cute. Precious, adorable, center of attention.

19

Perfectionist. Places high standards on himself, and often on others, desiring that everything be in proper order at all times.

Pleasant. Easy going, easy to be around, easy to talk with.

Productive. Must constantly be working or achieving, often finds it very difficult to rest.

Popular. Life of the party and therefore much desired as a party guest.

20

Bouncy. A bubbly, lively personality, full of energy.

Bold. Fearless, daring, forward, unafraid of risk.

Behaved. Consistently desires to conduct himself within the realm of what he feels is proper.

Balanced. Stable, middle of the road personality, not subject to sharp highs or lows.

WEAKNESSES

21

Blank. A person who shows little facial expression or emotion.

Bashful. Shrinks from getting attention, resulting from self-consciousness.

Brassy. Showy, flashy, comes on strong, too loud.

Bossy. Commanding, domineering, sometimes overbearing in adult relationships.

22

Undisciplined. A person whose lack of order permeates most every area of his life.

Unsympathetic. Finds it difficult to relate to the problems or hurts of others.

Unenthusiastic. Tends to not get excited, often feeling it won't work anyway.

Unforgiving. One who has difficulty forgiving or forgetting a hurt or injustice done to them, apt to hold onto a grudge.

23

Reticent. Unwilling or struggles against getting involved, especially when complex.

Resentful. Often holds ill feelings as a result of real or imagined offenses.

Resistant. Strives, works against, or hesitates to accept any other way but his own.

Repetitious. Retells stories and incidents to entertain you without realizing he has already told the story several times before, is constantly needing something to say.

24

Fussy. Insistent over petty matters or details, calling for great attention to trivial details.

Fearful. Often experiences feelings of deep concern, apprehension or anxiousness.

Forgetful. Lack of memory which is usually tied to a lack of discipline and not bothering to mentally record things that aren't fun.

Frank. Straightforward, outspoken, and doesn't mind telling you exactly what he thinks.

25

Impatient. A person who finds it difficult to endure irritation or wait for others.

Insecure. One who is apprehensive or lacks confidence.

Indecisive. The person who finds it difficult to make any decision at all. (Not the personality that labors long over each decision in order to make the perfect one.)

Interrupts. A person who is more of a talker than a listener, who starts speaking without even realizing someone else is already speaking.

26

Unpopular. A person whose intensity and demand for perfection can push others away.

Uninvolved. Has no desire to listen or become interested in clubs, groups, activities, or other people's lives.

Unpredictable. May be ecstatic one moment and down the next, or willing to help but then disappears, or promises to come but forgets to show up.

Unaffectionate. Finds it difficult to verbally or physically demonstrate tenderness openly.

27

Headstrong. Insists on having his own way.

Haphazard. Has no consistent way of doing things.

Hard to please. A person whose standards are set so high that it is difficult to ever satisfy them.

Hesitant. Slow to get moving and hard to get involved.

28

Plain. A middle-of-the-road personality without highs or lows and showing little, if any, emotion.

Pessimistic. While hoping for the best, this person generally sees the down side of a situation first.

Proud. One with great self-esteem who sees himself as always right and the best person for the job.

Permissive. Allows others (including children) to do as they please in order to keep from being disliked.

29

Angered easily. One who has a childlike flash-in-the-pan temper that expresses itself in tantrum style and is over and forgotten almost instantly.

Aimless. Not a goal-setter with little desire to be one.

Argumentative. Incites arguments generally because he is right no matter what the situation may be.

Alienated. Easily feels estranged from others, often because of insecurity or fear that others don't really enjoy his company.

30

Naive. Simple and child-like perspective, lacking sophistication or comprehension of what the deeper levels of life are really about.

Negative attitude. One whose attitude is seldom positive and is often able to see only the down or dark side of each situation.

Nervy. Full of confidence, fortitude, and sheer guts, often in a negative sense.

Nonchalant. Easy-going, unconcerned, indifferent.

31

Worrier. Consistently feels uncertain, troubled, or anxious.

Withdrawn. A person who pulls back to himself and needs a great deal of alone or isolation time.

Workaholic. An aggressive goal-setter who must be constantly productive and feels very guilty when resting, is not driven by a need for perfection or completion but by a need for accomplishment and reward.

Wants credit. Thrives on the credit or approval of others. As an entertainer this person feeds on the applause, laughter, and/or acceptance of an audience.

32

Too sensitive. Overly introspective and easily offended when misunderstood.

Tactless. Sometimes expresses himself in a somewhat offensive and inconsiderate way.

Timid. Shrinks from difficult situations.

Talkative. An entertaining, compulsive talker who finds it difficult to listen.

33

Doubtful. Characterized by uncertainty and lack of confidence that it will ever work out.

Disorganized. Lack of ability to ever get life in order.

Domineering. Compulsively takes control of situations and/or people, usually telling others what to do.

Depressed. A person who feels down much of the time.

34

Inconsistent. Erratic, contradictory, with actions and emotions not based on logic.

Introvert. A person whose thoughts and interest are directed inward, lives within himself.

Intolerant. Appears unable to withstand or accept another's attitudes, point of view or way of doing things.

Indifferent. A person to whom most things don't matter one way or the other.

35

Messy. Living in a state of disorder, unable to find things.

Moody. Doesn't get very high emotionlly, but easily slips into low lows, often when feeling unappreciated.

Mumbles. Will talk quietly under the breath when pushed, doesn't bother to speak clearly.

Manipulative. Influences or manages shrewdly or deviously for his own advantage, *will* get his way somehow.

36

Slow. Doesn't often act or think quickly, too much of a bother.

Stubborn. Determined to exert his or her own will, not easily persuaded, obstinate.

Show-off. Needs to be the center of attention, wants to be watched.

Skeptical. Disbelieving, questioning the motive behind the words.

37

Loner. Requires a lot of private time and tends to avoid other people.

Lord over. Doesn't hesitate to let you know that he is right or is in control.

Lazy. Evaluates work or activity in terms of how much energy it will take.

Loud. A person whose laugh or voice can be heard above others in the room.

38

Sluggish. Slow to get started, needs push to be motivated.

Suspicious. Tends to suspect or distrust others or ideas.

Short-tempered. Has a demanding impatience-based anger and a short fuse. Anger is expressed when others are not moving fast enough or have not completed what they have been asked to do.

Scatterbrained. Lacks the power of concentration, or attention, flighty.

39

Revengeful. Knowingly or otherwise holds a grudge and punishes the offender, often by subtly withholding friendship or affection.

Restless. Likes constant new activity because it isn't fun to do the same things all the time.

Reluctant. Unwilling or struggles against getting involved.

Rash. May act hastily, without thinking things through, generally because of impatience.

40

Compromising. Will often relax his position, even when right, in order to avoid conflict.

Critical. Constantly evaluating and making judgments, frequently thinking or expressing negative reactions.

Crafty. Shrewd, one who can always find a way to get to the desired end.

Changeable. A child-like, short attention span that needs a lot of change and variety to keep from getting bored.

APPENDIX C

Personality Summaries

Popular Sanguine Summary

Let's do it the fun way.

- Desire: Have fun
- Emotional needs: Attention, affection, approval, acceptance
- Key strengths: Can talk about anything at any time at any place with or without information. Has a bubbling personality, optimism, sense of humor, storytelling ability, likes people
- Key weaknesses: Disorganized, can't remember details or names, exaggerates, not serious about anything, trusts others to do the work, too gullible and naive
- Get depressed when: Life is no fun and no one seems to love them
- Are afraid of: Being unpopular or bored, having to live by the clock or keep a record of money spent
- Like people who: Listen and laugh, praise and approve
- Dislike people who: Criticize, don't respond to their humor, don't think they are cute
- Are valuable in work: For colorful creativity, optimism, light touch, cheering up others, entertaining
- Could improve if: They got organized, didn't talk so much and learned to tell time
- As leaders they: Excite, persuade and inspire others, exude charms and entertain, but are forgetful and poor on follow through
- Tend to marry: Perfect Melancholies who are sensitive and serious, but the Populars quickly tire of having to cheer them up all the time, and of being made to feel inadequate and stupid
- Reaction to stress: Leave the scene, go shopping, find a fun group, create excuses, blame others

- Recognized by: Constant talking, loud volume, bright eyes, moving hands, colorful expressions, enthusiasm, ability to mix easily

Perfect Melancholy Summary

Let's do it the right way.

- Desire: Have it right
- Emotional needs: Sense of stability, space, silence, sensitivity, and support
- Key strengths: Ability to organize, set long-range goals, have high standards and ideals, analyze deeply
- Key weaknesses: Easily depressed, too much time on preparation, too focused on details, remembers negatives, suspicious of others
- Get depressed when: Life is out of order, standards aren't met, and no one seems to care
- Are afraid of: No one understanding how they really feel, making mistakes, having to compromise standards
- Like people who: Are serious, intellectual, deep, and will carry on a sensible conversation
- Dislike people who: Are lightweights, forgetful, late, disorganized, superficial, prevaricating, and unpredictable
- Are valuable in work: For sense of details, love of analysis, follow through, high standards of performance, compassion for the hurting
- Could improve if: They didn't take life quite so seriously and didn't insist others be perfectionists
- As leaders they: Organize well, are sensitive to people's feelings, have deep creativity, want quality performance
- Tend to marry: Popular Sanguines for their personalities and social skills, but soon try to shut them up and get them on a schedule, becoming depressed when they don't respond
- Reaction to stress: Withdraw, get lost in a book, become depressed, give up, recount the problems
- Recognized by: Serious, sensitive nature, well-mannered approach, self-deprecating comments, meticulous and well-groomed looks (exceptions are hippy-type intellectuals, musicians, poets, who feel attention to clothes and looks is worldly and detracts from their inner strengths)

Powerful Choleric Summary

Let's do it my way.

- Desire: Have control
- Emotional needs: Sense of obedience, appreciation for accomplishments, credit for ability
- Key strengths: Ability to take charge of anything instantly, make quick, correct judgments
- Key weaknesses: Too bossy, domineering, autocratic, insensitive, impatient, unwilling to delegate or give credit to others
- Get depressed when: Life is out of control and people won't do things their way
- Are afraid of: Losing control of anything, such as losing a job, not being promoted, becoming seriously ill, having a rebellious child or unsupportive mate
- Like people who: Are supportive and submissive, see things their way, cooperate quickly, and let them take credit
- Dislike people who: Are lazy and not interested in working constantly, who buck their authority, get independent, or aren't loyal
- Are valuable in work: Because they can accomplish more than anyone else in a shorter time and are usually right, but may stir up trouble
- Could improve if: They allowed others to make decisions, delegated authority, became more patient, didn't expect everyone to produce as they do
- As leaders they: Have a natural feel for being in charge, a quick sense of what will work, and a sincere belief in their ability to achieve but may overwhelm less aggressive people
- Tend to marry: Peaceful Melancholies who will quietly obey and not buck their authority, but who never accomplish enough or get excited over their projects
- Reaction to stress: Tighten control, work harder, exercise more, get rid of offender
- Recognized by: Fast-moving approach, quick grab for control, self-confidence, restless and overpowering attitude

Peaceful Phlegmatic Summary

Let's do it the easy way.

- Desire: Have no conflict, keep peace
- Emotional needs: Sense of respect, feeling of worth, understanding, emotional support
- Key strengths: Balance, even disposition, dry sense of humor, pleasing personality
- Key weaknesses: Lack of decisiveness, enthusiasm, and energy, no obvious flaws but a hidden will of iron
- Get depressed when: Life is full of conflict, they have to face a personal confrontation, no one wants to help, the buck stops with them
- Are afraid of: Having to deal with a major personal problem, being left holding the bag, making major changes
- Like people who: Will make decisions for them, will recognize their strengths, will not ignore them, will give them respect
- Dislike people who: Are too pushy, too loud, and expect too much of them
- Are valuable in work: Because they cooperate and are a calming influence, keep peace, mediate between contentious people, objectively solve problems
- Could improve if: They set goals and became self-motivated, they were willing to do more and move faster than expected, and could face their own problems as well as they handle other peoples'
- As leaders they: Keep calm, cool, and collected, don't make impulsive decisions, are well-liked and inoffensive, won't cause trouble, but don't often come up with brilliant new ideas
- Tend to marry: Powerful Cholerics because they respect their strength and decisiveness, but later the Peacefuls get tired of being pushed around and looked down upon
- Reaction to stress: Hide from it, watch television, eat, tune out on life
- Recognized by: Calm approach, relaxed posture, sitting or leaning when possible

Reprinted from *Personalities in Power,* published by Huntington House Inc., P.O. Box 53788 Lafayette, LA. 70505.

Valuable Resources

Resources in Building Your Reservoir of Personalities Knowledge

All of the following books are by Florence Littauer except where indicated.

Personalities for Fun

Personality Plus, Fleming H. Revell; Florence's humorous and best selling book on the strengths and weaknesses of the four personalities.

Personality Plus, book and tape kit, CLASS Book Service; includes book, two extra tests, and Florence's fun filled day-long seminar (four audio tapes)

Personalities in Depth

Your Personality Tree, Word Books; Florence's classic advanced book, dealing with the masks we often wear, our emotional needs, and how childhood experiences affect our present personality

Your Personality Tree, video and book album, Word Books; includes book, 8½ hour video Cassons (two cassettes), and Study Guide

Personalities in Leadership

Personalities in Power, The Making of Great Leaders, Huntington House; Florence uses the presidents of the United States, from Franklin Roosevelt to George Bush, to show that each personality can be a leader, showing how each one succeeded in his strengths and struggled in his areas of personality weaknesses

Personalities for Motivation

Dare to Dream, Word Books; Florence's challenging book that will help you to fulfill your life's aspirations, with a valuable section on "Repairing Your Dream" when you encounter detours or roadblocks on your journey to success

Personalities in Words of Encouragement

Silver Boxes, The Gift of Encouragement, Word Books; how the spoken words can give a lift and belief in one's self, or may tear down for all time a person's self-confidence in the ability to achieve

Silver Boxes, audio message, Word Books; highly acclaimed and deeply moving (audio tape)

Personalities with Children

Raising Christians, not Just Children, Word Books; a practical guide and timely tips for successfully raising children at all ages, with a complete section on understanding and dealing with your children's personalities when they are totally unlike yours

Personalities in Church

How to Get Along with Difficult People, Harvest House; sixteen different characters—you've probably met in church: Sam Sermon, Bob Bossy, Joyce Judging, Gilda Guilt, and others. Why they're difficult and what you can do to get along with them

Personalities and Emotional Pain

Freeing Your Mind from Memories That Bind, Thomas Nelson Publishers; powerful best-selling book that will help you uncover and understand how your childhood experiences may have altered your birth personality and may still be affecting who you are today. Coauthored with Fred Littauer

The Promise of Restoration, Thomas Nelson Publishers; companion book to *Freeing Your Mind. . . .* Leads you in the important steps of complete recovery. By Fred Littauer

Personalities in Marriage

After Every Wedding Comes a Marriage, Harvest House; valuable insights to a successful marriage, including understanding and accepting each other's personality differences

Remarried with Children, Thomas Nelson Publishers; practical and poignant tools for making a blended family work by two who did; includes an understanding of the personalities and increases the hopes for success. By Don and LaDean Houck

Personalities in Times of Grief

Roses in December, Thomas Nelson Publishers; a touching book on dealing with grief by an author and speaker who has lost three children at separate times. Shows how different personalities handle grief. By Marilyn Heavilin

Help in Other Situations of Life

Help in Overcoming Depression

Blow Away the Black Clouds, Harvest House; a woman's answer to depression—help for overcoming and understanding the symptoms in plain layman's terms

Help in Women's Ministries

Giving Back, Thomas Nelson Publishers; an excellent and helpful book to give you practical ideas to make your corner of the world a little bit better. By Marita Littauer

Help in Family Creativity

Home Made Memories, Harvest House; shows you how to make meal times and holidays experiences that your children will never want to forget. By Marita Littauer

Help in Life's Disappointments

Make the Tough Times Count: How to Rise Above Adversity, Thomas Nelson Publishers; Florence did and shows you how you can, too, in a book you won't be able to put down

Hope for Hurting Women, Word Books; inspiring stories of fifteen women who overcame severe hurdles to success and fulfillment, showing how you can as well

It Takes So Little to Be Above Average, Harvest House; how to move beyond the middle lane of life—with a little extra effort you can rise to the top

For further information, contact:
CLASS Book Service
1645 S. Rancho Sante Fe Road #102
San Marcos, CA 92069
(800) 433-6633

If you wish information on speaking availability of either Florence or Marita Littauer call (619) 471-1722.